CHILD'S PLAY

CHILD'S PLAY

200
INSTANT CRAFTS
AND ACTIVITIES
FOR
PRESCHOOLERS

Leslie Hamilton

Crown Publishers, Inc.
New York

Publisher's Note: As the possibility exists for injury in any playtime activity, all activities described in this book should be supervised by a responsible adult.

Published by Crown Publishers, Inc., 201 East 50th Street, New York, New York 10022

CROWN is a trademark of Crown Publishers, Inc.

Manufactured in the United States of America

Design by Lauren Dong

Library of Congress Cataloging-in-Publication Data

Hamilton, Leslie
    Child's play : 200 instant crafts and activities for preschoolers/Leslie Hamilton.
    Includes index.
    Summary: A collection of 200 crafts, games, and activities, including things to make from paper, egg cartons, and cloth, science and writing projects, recipes, quiet games, and games to play in the car.
    1. Handicraft — Juvenile literature. 2. Creative activities and seat work — Juvenile literature. [1. Handicraft. 2. Games.] I. Title.
    TT160.H33   1989
    790.1'922 — dc 19   88-26901

ISBN 0-517-57171-4

10 9 8 7 6 5 4 3

First Edition

To Larry, Sarah, and David
with love

CONTENTS

PROJECTS AND ACTIVITIES — 55

CARDBOARD TUBE CRAFTS

EGG-CARTON CRAFTS

SCIENCE PROJECTS — 75

ACKNOWLEDGMENTS

A small group of very special people helped me put this book together. I would like to thank them here:

My husband, Larry, with never-ending patience, gave me support, encouragement, and invaluable guidance as I learned the complexities of our word processor. Without him, this book would still be a pile of index cards.

My children, Sarah and David, were enthusiastic participants and critics as I recorded activities both old and new. It is because of them and their wonderful desire to learn and do new things that this book was written.

I am especially grateful to my early reviewers, Beryl Anderson, Vivian Pearlman, Barbara Hobson, Lidia Garbach, and Wendy Harris. Many of their comments and suggestions were incorporated into the book and are lovingly appreciated.

Others who helped with comments or ideas were Jenna Hutchinson, Alicita Hamilton, Ilana Hobson, Sandy Johnson, Karen Vawter, and Barb Calhoun.

My editor, Barbara Grossman, showed heroic patience, understanding, and humor as she coped with my insecurities and long lists of questions.

And finally, a loving thank you to my parents, Judith and Sholom Pearlman, who raised their seven children with creativity, humor, and love.

A NOTE TO PARENTS AND CAREGIVERS

Child's Play is a collection of crafts, projects, and games geared mainly toward children eighteen months to six years old. All of these projects are *quick and easy*—no waiting for things to dry, set, rise, or whatever. These are ideas for instant entertainment and fun; a fast release from boredom on a housebound day. Happily, most of these projects have a very minimal "mess factor," and are easily cleaned up by a child and/or an adult in minutes.

All of the activities mentioned in *Child's Play* are inexpensive or completely free. Many of the projects use things you normally throw away (see Basic Supplies, page xix). You and your child are encouraged to use the resources at hand, to take a closer look at your surroundings and use what you find for fun.

Encourage your child to use his or her creativity. Often, the simplest idea can blossom into an hour's entertainment. All that is needed is a supportive adult (with a sense of humor), a suggestion or two, and a child's imagination.

CHOOSING PROJECTS FOR YOUR CHILD

To make choosing your child's activities easier, each craft or project is labeled with one or more symbols. The symbols suggest an *approximate* age level for the activity, and an idea of how closely supervised your child should be.

● marks an activity appropriate for toddlers—children 1½ to 3 years who are just learning coloring and scissors skills. While ● crafts require lots of adult help, they ask for little in the way of a child's patience. Often, an adult or an older child will do much of the actual work, with help from the toddler, who can then play with the results.

■ projects are for the slightly more advanced child, roughly 2½ to 4½ years, who has a greater mastery of skills and a longer attention span than the toddler.

▲ activities are for the "senior citizen" of the preschool crowd, the 4- to 6-year-old. These activities require a bit more patience and attention from the child, and mastery of certain skills. These children are able to continue many projects on their own, and then improve on or expand the original idea.

Most of the activities are marked ●■, ■▲, or ●■▲. These projects appeal to children of mixed ages and abilities. The big difference here is how much adult supervision and help are required. Sometimes the happy result is that an older child can help the younger child, and both are entertained.

Finally, there is a caution symbol: ! This is simply a reminder to take a bit more care during the activity. Constant adult supervision is suggested when young children are in the kitchen. Pot handles should be turned toward the back of the stove to avoid spills. Remind children that metal spoons get hot when left in a hot pan, and hot air comes out of hot ovens.

BASIC SUPPLIES

This is a list of supplies most often required for the arts and crafts projects in *Child's Play*. Most, if not all, of the following will be things you already have in your home.

Work surface—An old plastic tablecloth, plastic placemats, a sheet of plastic, a broken window shade, or newspaper (if you don't mind the ink smudges). Anything to protect your furniture from glue drips or crayon marks.

White paper—Paper is expensive, so think about recycling! Use the blank sides of junk mail, computer paper, mimeo mistakes from a local grade school. Large newsprint pads are sometimes available at stores or newspaper offices at low cost. Freezer paper is great for *big* drawings.

Colored construction paper—Or use recycled gift-wrap paper or wallpaper samples.

Clear Con-Tact paper—self-adhesive paper, sold in rolls or by the yard. Available in hardware and department stores. Optional, but nice to have.

Tape—clear, masking.

Glue—nontoxic; or use paste or a glue stick.

Old magazines and/or catalogs—Save the ones with lots of brightly colored pictures.

Crayons—nontoxic.

Felt-tipped markers—nontoxic and washable. These aren't necessary, but the colors are beautiful, and they're fun to use.

Pencils—for older children.

Scissors—Try to find blunt-tipped scissors that *really* cut.

Paints—watercolors, poster paints.

Miscellaneous Throwaways or Household Items—plastic milk jugs or other plastic bottles; wax paper; aluminum foil; paper cups; egg cartons; paper plates; egg shells; peanut shells; cardboard boxes (shoe boxes, big boxes, tiny boxes, round oatmeal boxes); cardboard tubes from paper towels, toilet paper, gift wrap; Styrofoam meat or vegetable trays; broken crayons; paper bags; drinking straws; kitchen utensils; etc.

SUPERFAST
~ PAPER ~
# PROJECTS

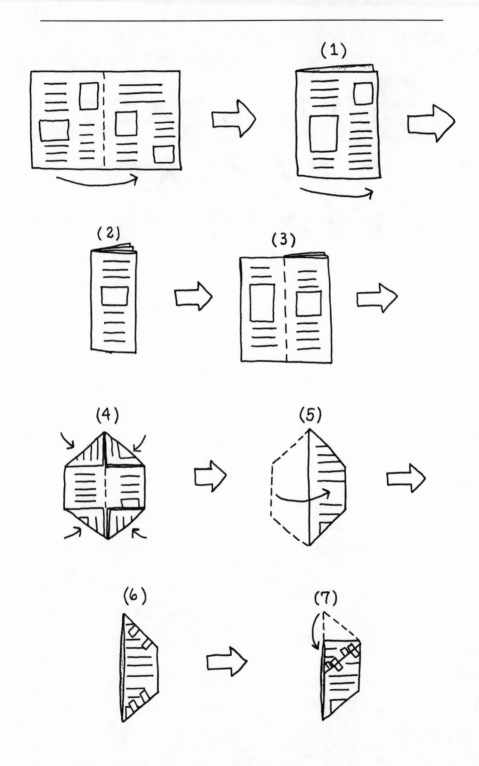

●■▲ NEWSPAPER HAT

You need: 2-page sheet of newspaper
Tape
Crayons or markers (optional)

You do: (See diagram.)
Fold newspaper in half along fold line. (1)
Fold in half again. (2)
Open one quarter of page out and lay, folds down, on work surface. (3)
Fold back corners to center fold line. (4)
Fold in half with corners inside. (5)
Tape diagonal edges to hold together. (6)
Fold one end over and tape. (7)

Child does: Helps with folding.
Puts on tape.
Decorates.
Wears forward for adventurer, or backward for fire-hat.

● ■ ▲　**SNAPPY PUPPET MOUTHS**

This is tricky the first time, but, once mastered, takes only one minute to make.

You need:　Square piece of paper (any size)
　　　　　　　Scissors (optional)
　　　　　　　Crayon, marker, pencil

You do:　　(See diagram.)
　　　　　　Fold paper in half. (1)
　　　　　　Fold in half again, in same direction. (2)
　　　　　　Open one quarter of page out and lay, folds down, on work surface. (3)
　　　　　　Fold corners back to center fold line. (4)
　　　　　　Fold in half, along center fold line, with corners inside. (5)
　　　　　　Fold tip to tip and make a small crease on the fold, as shown in diagram. (6)
　　　　　　Unfold and make a ½-inch cut or tear, through all layers, at crease. (7)
　　　　　　Make four "lips" by folding back from cut, tapering to points. Fold back two lips on one side of puppet, then flip over and fold back other two lips. (8)
　　　　　　Open up by pulling apart at cut, and bending points to touch each other. (9)
　　　　　　Operate by holding gently in hand, thumb under "mouth." Mouth will snap open and shut. (10)

Child does:　Decorates with eyes, nose, hair.
　　　　　　　Holds puppet conversations. (These puppets are famous for nose pinching! They are also very hungry and like to eat small things.)

(1)

(2)

(3)

(4)

(5)

(6)
crease

(7)

(8)
Side One   Side Two

(9)

(10)

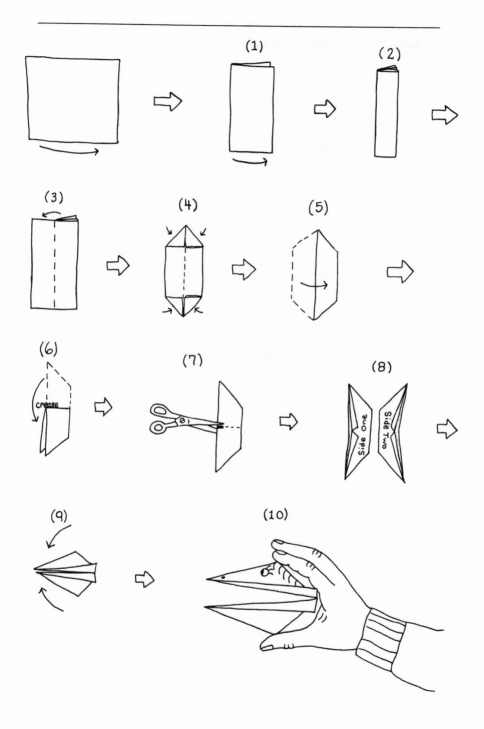

●■▲ PAPER HELICOPTER

You need: Rectangular paper (any size)
1–2 paper clips or tape
Scissors

You do: (See diagram.)
Fold paper in half and then unfold. (1)
Cut out three triangles, as shown in diagram. (2)
Cut down center of paper to fold line. Cut side triangles in a little more. (3)
Fold bottom paper in thirds and secure with paper clip or tape. Fold one upper flap forward and one back at new fold line. (4)

Note: If helicopter doesn't fly well, add more tape or another paper clip to the bottom.

Child does: Helps with folding.
Stands on a chair and drops helicopter.
Decorates helicopter.

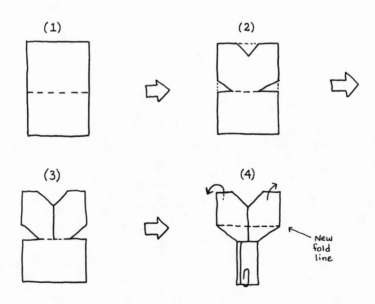

▲ PAPER AIRPLANE

You need: Rectangular paper
Crayons or markers

You and   (See diagram.)
child do: Fold paper in half, the long way. (1)
Unfold paper. Now it has a fold line down the middle. (2)
Fold two corners in, to meet at the fold line. (3)
Fold *those* folds in, to meet at the fold line. (4)
Fold the plane in half on the fold line. All folds should be inside. (5)
Fold each edge back out to the big fold. (6)

Child does: Decorates and flies plane. (7)

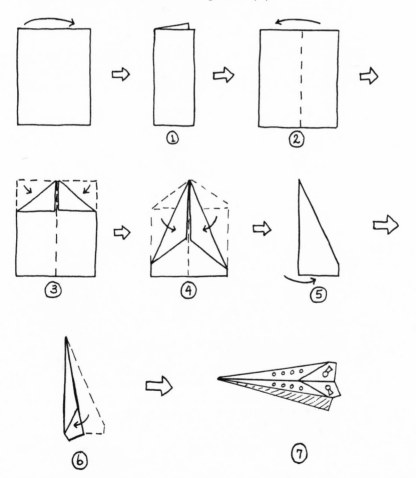

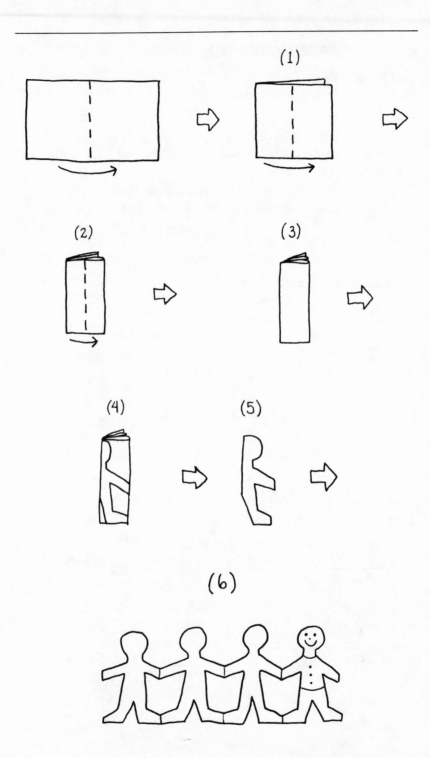

▲ GIANT PAPER DOLLS

(Giant dolls are easier to cut out and decorate.)

You need: Lightweight paper (a nice size is 8½ × 11 inches or bigger)
Scissors
Crayons, markers, pencils

You do: (See diagram.)
Fold paper in half the short way. (1)
Fold in half again, in same direction. (2) (For only two paper dolls, stop folding here.)
Fold in half again, in same direction. (3)
Draw half shape of doll on folded paper, with center of head at big fold and arms and feet extending all the way out to the opposite edges. (4)
Cut out half doll through all layers. (5)

Note: If dolls fall apart when unfolded, try again and make sure that hands and feet extend all the way to the edge of the paper.

Child does: Decides if dolls have skirts or pants.
Older child can cut along predrawn cutting line (make only two dolls).
Unfolds dolls. (6)
Decorates with faces, clothes, hair.

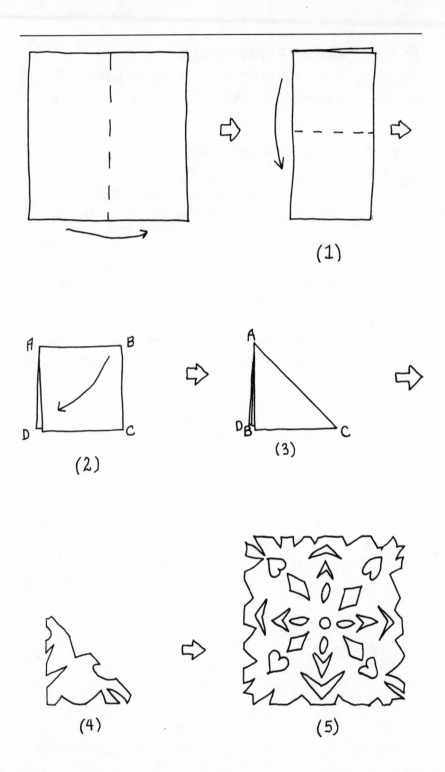

(1)

A   B

D   C

(2)

A

D B   C

(3)

(4)

(5)

■▲ PAPER SNOWFLAKES

You need: Square lightweight paper (any size)—junk mail, newsprint, paper napkins, etc.
Scissors

You do: (See diagram.)
Fold square in half. (1)
Fold in half downwards. (2)
Fold in half diagonally, so that corner B meets corner D. (3)
With scissors, round corner C and cut small wedges and triangles out of all three sides. Snip off corner A. (4)

Child does: Helps with folding.
Shows where to cut wedges.
Unfolds snowflake. (5)
Glues snowflake to paper backing of a different color.
Or hangs snowflake from a thread.
Or tapes snowflake in window.

●■▲ PAPER FAN

You need: Rectangular paper, white or colored
Crayons or markers
Tape

Child does: Draws any type of picture or design on one or both sides of paper.

You and (See diagram.)
child do: Make 1-inch folds, back and forth, in paper, as shown. (1)
At one end, gather folds and tape together to form handle. (2)

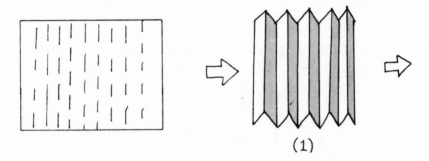

(1)

(2)

●■▲   SMALL OBJECT RUBBINGS

You need: White paper (blank side of junk mail is fine)
Crayon or pencil (not marker)
Small objects to "rub" (coins, bobby pin, car key, paper clip, checker, button, etc. Anything reasonably flat with an interesting texture.)

You do: Tape corners of paper to work surface.

Child does: Slides the first object under the paper.
Lightly rubs over the object with crayon or pencil. The texture and shape of the object will appear.

Ideas: ● Very young children will need help, and may enjoy simply watching the rubbed objects appear on the paper as you do the rubbing. Play a guessing game, and let your child guess what the object is as its pattern appears on the paper.
■▲ Older children can do the rubbings themselves. After child has made between six and ten rubbings on one page, collect objects and let child match them to the rubbed pattern, in a matching game.

●■▲ TRACING, SMALL SCALE

You need: White paper (blank side of junk mail is fine)
Pencil
Small objects (kitchen utensils, cups, coins, spoons, small toys, puzzle pieces, cookie cutters, etc.)
Crayons or markers
Scissors (optional)

You do: Tape paper to work surface.
Help younger child to trace around objects, either one or many to a page.

Child does: Chooses objects to be traced.
Colors tracings.
●■ Plays matching game, fitting objects onto their traced patterns.
▲ Older children can do the tracing themselves, and might want to cut out the traced shapes to be glued on colored paper as a collage.

■▲ TRACING, MEDIUM SCALE

You need: White paper (big enough for objects to be traced)
Pencil
Markers, crayons
Scissors (optional)
Toys (dolls, stuffed animals, trucks, a shoe, child's hand, etc.)

You do: Tape paper to work surface.
Help child trace around object, if needed.

Child does: Traces object.
Colors and decorates tracing: face and clothes on doll; wheels and doors on truck; rings and bracelet or watch on hand. (See examples.)
Cuts out tracings to mount on colored paper if desired.

14

TRACING

TRACING YOUR CHILD

●■▲   TRACING YOUR CHILD

You need: Large, blank paper. (Use computer paper, white side of recycled wrapping paper, freezer paper, 2–3 grocery bags opened up and taped together, or sheets of plain paper taped together.)
Markers or crayons

You do: Have child lie on his/her back on the paper.
Trace around the child, paying careful attention to ears, hair, fingers, braids, and any special details.

Child does: Colors in his/her own face, clothes, etc. Don't forget freckles, jewelry, etc., or draw in a costume.
Cuts out, if desired.
Tapes to door for life-size decoration.

■▲   COOPERATIVE PICTURE

You need: White paper
Crayon, marker, or pencil
2 or more people

You and child do: You draw small part of picture and explain what you drew (e.g., "I drew somebody's tummy.").
Child draws addition to your picture and explains it ("I drew the arms.").
Continue alternating until child decides that picture is finished.
Two or more older children can do this without any help from adults.

■▲   MAP MAKING

You need: Paper
Crayons, markers, or pencils

You and   (See examples.)
child do: Make a map of a familiar place:
● your child's bedroom
● one level of your house or apartment
● a section of your neighborhood
● a trip to a familiar place (school, grocery store, etc.).

Note: Accuracy and scale are not important at all. Just try for the general idea of your surroundings. Include furniture, rugs, doorways on indoor maps; parking lots, trees, buildings on outdoor maps. Let your child decide what landmarks are important.

You can label the objects and places on the map, or leave them blank. Your child can color the map if he/she wants to.

●■▲　MAP ACTIVITY #1—Pretend Town

You need:　Large paper (preferably 3 × 3 feet or bigger)
Clear Con-Tact paper (optional)
Small toy cars, people, airplanes, etc.

You and
child do:　(See example.)
Map a pretend (or real) town on a scale large enough for toy cars to fit on the streets and toy people to walk "into" the buildings. Include roads, stores, airports, railroad tracks, parking lots, gas stations, a pond, etc.

Child does:　Colors in map, if desired.

You do:　Cover with clear Con-Tact paper to make the map more durable.

Ideas:　Have pretend trips to school or to the airport. Create pretend traffic jams or have a fire truck rushing to a fire.
On the same large scale, map a wilderness area with lakes, rivers, mountains, trails, log bridges, and caves. Toy people can hike the trails, searching for adventure.

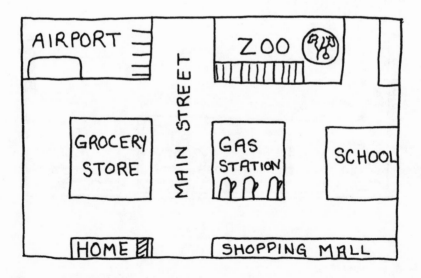

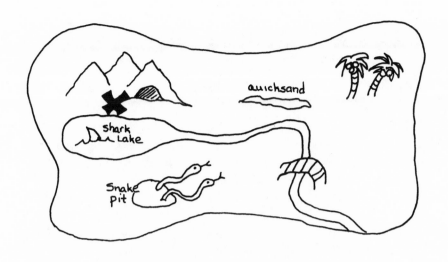

■▲   MAP ACTIVITY #2—Treasure Map

You need: Plain white paper (8 × 11 inches) or brown paper
         bag
         Markers (best) or crayons

You do: Cut paper into treasure map shape. (See example.)
         Optional: If using white paper, *carefully* scorch edges
            and *lightly* brown paper over stove burner, for
            authentic aged look.

Child does: (See example.)
         (Younger child will need help; older child will make
            a better map than you will.)
         Makes a map of an imaginary treasure island, com-
            plete with palm trees, bridges, rivers, caves, moun-
            tains, dangerous animals, and a large *X* marking
            the spot.
         Rolls it up and hides it in a safe spot, or mounts it on
            a wall. This is a good activity while playing pirates.

■▲ MAP ACTIVITY #3—Draw What You See/Saw

You need: White paper
Crayon, markers, pencil
A trip, before or after

You and child do: Make a map before, during, or after going on a short trip (to the store, park, friend's house, etc.).

If mapping the trip beforehand, let child hold map and be Navigator, keeping track of where you're going and what comes next. Or on return from a trip, have child map where he/she has just been ("Draw what you saw.").

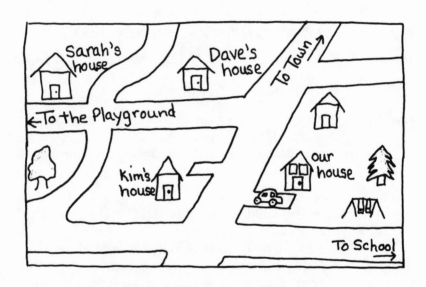

▲ MAP ACTIVITY #4—Treasure Hunt

You need: A simple map of the room you are in

You do: Hide a small object (could be a snack) in the room and mark its location on the map.

Child does: Using the map as a guide, child hunts for "treasure."

■▲ PAPER COLLAGES

You need: Paper for background (black is nice)
Paper collage materials: scraps of colored paper, torn
  or cut; pictures from magazines; colored circles
  made with a paper punch, etc.
White glue, paste, or glue stick
Clear Con-Tact paper (optional)

You do: Pour a small amount of glue onto a square of paper
or aluminum foil. Child can put glue on paper
pieces or background using a toothpick (for small
pieces), a Popsicle stick, or a stiff scrap of paper.
This method eliminates the prevalent overgluing
problem.

Child does: Helps gather or cut up scraps.
Glues scraps to paper.

Ideas: Crazy room collage: Cut out pictures of furniture and
glue them onto background to make a regular or
funny room.
Crazy people collage: Cut out pictures of faces,
clothes, shoes, etc., and glue on paper to make
composite person.
Toy collage: Good use for all those toy catalogs that
come in the mail. Cut out lots of pictures of
favorite toys and glue on paper.

Note: For permanent paper placemat, cover collage with
clear Con-Tact paper when glue is dry.

● LEARNING SCISSORS SKILLS

You need: Scissors
Junk mail, catalog pages, coupon pages, etc.

You and   With child on your lap, let child do the cutting
child do: (random) while *you* hold the paper. This is a nice
way for a young child to learn about and enjoy
working with scissors, without getting cut. As
he/she gains skills, try cutting out coupons or
following straight lines.

■▲ WEAVING PAPER PLACEMATS

You need: Colored construction paper
Scissors
Tape
Clear Con-Tact paper (optional)

You do: (See diagram.)
Fold one piece of construction paper in half and draw cutting lines, as shown.
Cut strips of paper about 1 inch wide for weaving.
Explain weaving process to child, but don't expect perfect results.

Child does: Helps cut strips of paper.
Cuts slits on cutting lines.
Weaves paper strips in and out, securing ends with tape.

Note: For permanent placemat, cover finished mat with clear Con-Tact paper.

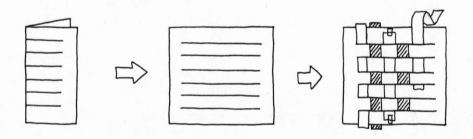

■▲ PARTY DECORATIONS

You need: Construction paper
Scissors
Clear tape
Crayons or markers

You and child do: First, let your child know that the party (for children or adults) will be even better with some home-made decorations and name tags for the table.

Name Tags—Cut construction paper squares about 3 × 3 inches and fold them in half. On the front of each, help child write a guest's name and draw a design. Children can put one tag at each place at the table.

Other Decorations—Trace and cut out oak or maple leaves, and tape them to windows.

Make paper chains from loops of paper.

Hang paper snowflakes from the ceiling.

Make paper jack o' lanterns, snowmen, candles, etc., using the theme of the party for ideas.

Make paper cutouts of balloons and attach yarn for "string." Hang on windows or walls.

Hang Japanese Lanterns (see following page).

▲ JAPANESE LANTERNS

You need: Rectangular paper (colored or white)
Scissors
Tape

You do: (See diagram.)
Fold paper in half the long way.
Draw cutting lines (if necessary) about an inch apart, stopping at least an inch from the edge of the paper.

Child does: Cuts on cutting lines.

You and (See diagram.)
child do: Open paper and bring Side A over to Side B. Overlap edges a bit and tape together at top and bottom.
Make a hanger or handle by taping a strip of paper (any color) to the top.

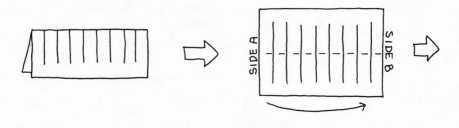

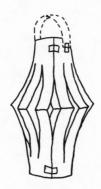

SEWING AND WEAVING

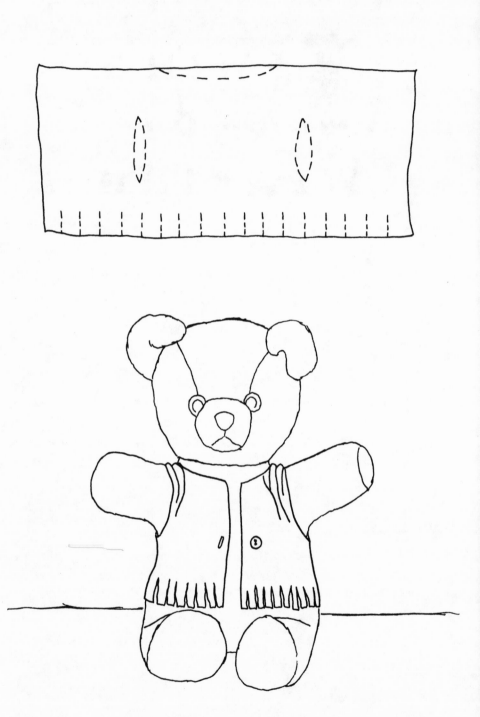

Children can use fabric cut from old clothes ready for the scrap heap. Use leftovers from a larger sewing project, or make a trip to a fabric store to find treasures in the remnant piles.

●■▲ NO-SEW VEST

You need: Fabric large enough to wrap around stuffed animal or doll
Scissors
Pencil

You and child do: (See illustration.)
Wrap fabric around stuffed animal and approximate where armholes should go.
Have child mark armholes with pencil.
Cut slits or narrow holes to fit animal's arms.
Cut curve for animal's neck.
If desired, cut fringe along bottom edge of vest.
Have child dress animal.
(For a finishing touch, a button can be added to the front, with a tiny cut for the buttonhole.)

● ■ ▲   NO-SEW SUPER CAPE

You need: Newspaper for pattern
Scissors
Crayon
Fabric (Felt works especially well.)

You and   (See diagram.)
child do: Estimate how large the cape needs to be. For a
12-inch stuffed animal, the cape should be about 7
inches long and 6 inches wide, and the ties should
each be 12 inches long. So you would need a piece
of newspaper that is 19 inches long and 6 inches
wide.

Draw and cut a large U-shape out of the correct size
piece of newspaper. (1)

Bring the ties around the stuffed animal's neck to see
if they are long enough to tie (or tape) in front. (2)

Adjust or trim newspaper pattern.

Cut out fabric cape, using pattern.

Decorate.

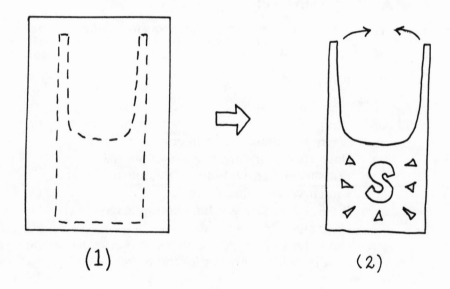

(1)   (2)

●■   THREADING OBJECTS—No Needle

You need: A piece of yarn, about 2 feet long
Objects to thread: Cheerios, macaroni shapes
Tape

You do: Wrap one end of yarn with a bit of tape, to make
threading easier.
Tie the other end of the yarn to one of the threading
objects, so that things won't fall off the yarn.

Child does: Child can thread Cheerios, macaroni, or both, and
make a necklace or decoration.

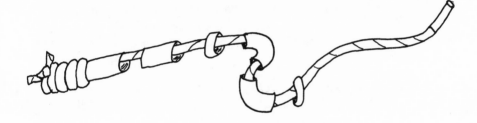

●■   Also try **Spaghetti Threader Game,** (page 141).

29

■▲ SEWING CARDS

You need: Thin cardboard, large or small (Good sources: paper plates, backs of note pads, cardboard from tights or stockings package, large index cards)
Sharp pencil
Markers or crayons
A piece of yarn, about 2–3 feet long
Clear tape

You do: (See examples.)
Draw a simple line drawing. Straight lines are best.
Using a pencil (or paper punch), punch holes in the drawing at corners, angles, or wherever.
Thread one end of yarn through a hole near cardboard edge, and tie it to the card.
Wrap a bit of tape around the other end of the yarn, to make threading easier.

Child does: Suggests the picture for the card.
Sews in-and-out stitch in any pattern, or following the lines of the drawing.

Note: A collection of these makes a great, nonmessy, portable toy for the car.
The cardboard cards will last longer if you cover them with clear Con-Tact paper before punching the holes.

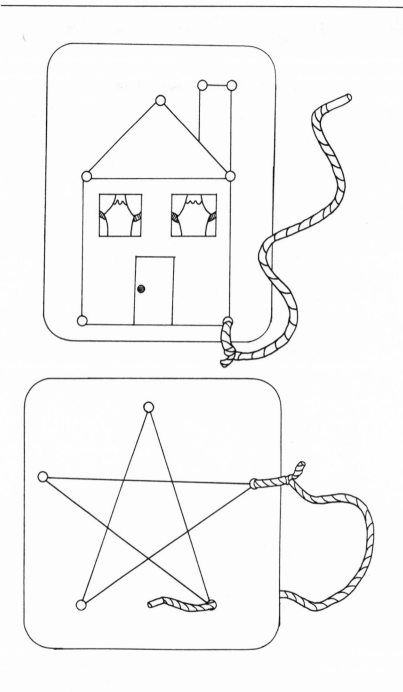

▲ THREADING OBJECTS—Needle and Thread

You need: Large needle with doubled thread about 2 feet long. (A needle about 2 inches long is a good size for little hands.)

Objects to thread: Styrofoam packing pieces, popped popcorn, buttons, cranberries

You do: Make a big knot in the end of the thread and start child off with two or three threaded objects.

Child does: Threads objects to make a necklace or decoration.

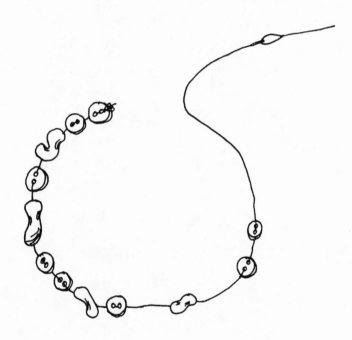

▲ SIMPLE SCARF FOR STUFFED ANIMAL OR DOLL

You need: Scarf-sized fabric for animal or doll (about 2 inches wide and about 6–12 inches long)

Scissors

Needle

Thread of contrasting color to fabric. Doubled thread should be about 6 inches longer than scarf.

You and child do: (See diagram.)

Cut scarf to correct size and shape.

Cut short fringes on ends of scarf.

Thread needle and knot ends together.

Start child off doing in-and-out (running) stitches down the middle of the scarf, as decoration.

Child does: Chooses fabric and contrasting color of thread.

Idea: Try making a matching scarf and vest, using the No-Sew Vest pattern, page 27.

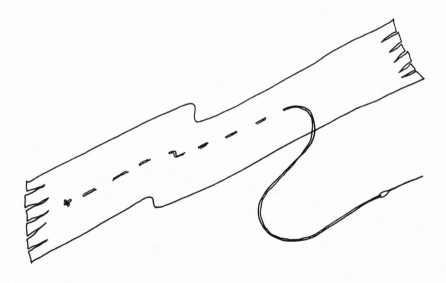

▲ BEAN BAGS

You need: 2 squares of different color fabric (5 × 5 inches approximately)
Needle and thread
Dry beans, rice, or popcorn

*You and
child do:* (See diagram.)
With right sides of fabric together, sew around all edges, leaving a 2-inch space to pour in the beans. (1)
To reinforce a simple running stitch, you or child can go back over stitches, filling in spaces, as shown. (2)
Turn fabric right side out and fill with beans, rice, or popcorn. (3)
Sew up 2-inch space, using a whipstitch. (4)

● ■ ▲ BEAN BAG GAMES

Heads or Tails
Toss two-color bean bag in the air and have child guess which color will land facing up.

Tricky Catch
Play catch using two hands, then only one hand, then have child catch bean bag using a large plastic bowl or a gallon milk jug with the top cut off.

Bean Bag Basketball
Toss the bean bag into a big pot on the floor, starting close up and taking a step backward after each successful "basket."

Bean Bag Crawl
Put bean bag on child's back and see how far he/she can crawl before it falls off.

Bean Bag Walk
Child balances bean bag on head as he/she walks, sits in a chair, sits on floor, walks backward, etc.

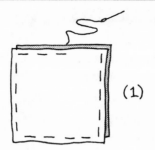

(1)

(2) **To reinforce stitch:**

sew in one direction first,   **and then reverse direction to fill in the spaces.**

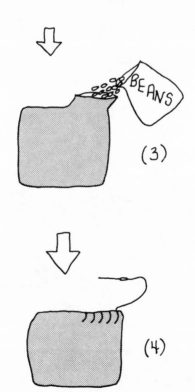

(3)

(4)

▲   LITTLE PILLOWS

You need: 2 squares or rectangles of fabric, slightly larger than desired pillow size
Needle and thread
Cotton balls, old stockings, or other suitable stuffing

Child does: Chooses fabric.
Chooses size of pillow.
Chooses doll or stuffed animal to receive pillow.

You and child do: With right sides of fabric together, sew edges all around, leaving a 2-inch space on one edge.
Turn right side out.
Stuff with cotton balls or other stuffing material.
Sew pillow closed, using whipstitch.

COTTON BALLS

■▲ STYROFOAM TRAY WEAVING

You need: Styrofoam food tray from meat or vegetables
Sharp knife
Construction paper strips or ribbon scraps
Tape

You do: (See illustration.)
Thoroughly wash Styrofoam tray. (Let child dry it.)
On cutting board, cut slits in tray, as shown.

Child does: Cuts paper strips (about ¾–1 inch wide).
Weaves strips into tray, securing ends with tape.

Note: This is a timely activity during dinner preparation.

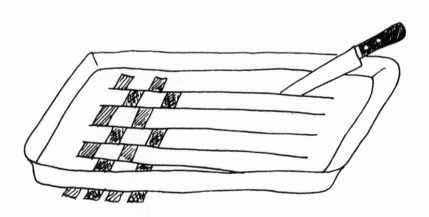

▲ BERRY BOX WEAVING

You need: A plastic berry box (Grocery stores sell either berries or cherry tomatoes in square plastic boxes. They give them away for the asking.)

Ribbon, recycled gift ribbon, thin strips of fabric, yarn, or paper strips

Tape (if using paper strips)

You and (See illustration.)
child do: Weave ribbon, yarn, etc., in and out of the spaces in the box, securing ends by tying (or taping, if using paper strips).

Put a square of cloth or paper inside the bottom of the box.

If desired, make a handle using ribbon, gift ribbon or a pipe cleaner.

Fill box with treasures or treats.

Note: This makes a nice gift for Mother's Day, Father's Day, etc., or a homemade Easter basket.

It is also an inexpensive and easy group project.

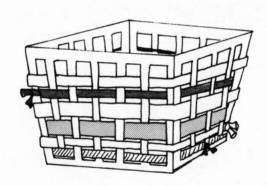

■▲   Also try **Weaving Paper Placemats,** page 22.

BOXES

All types of cardboard boxes are useful, so save round oatmeal boxes; shoe boxes; small, medium, and large corrugated cardboard boxes; and giant boxes from large appliances.

OATMEAL BOX CRAFTS

●■▲ TOY TRUCK TUNNEL

You need: Round oatmeal box (lid not needed)
Heavy scissors or knife
Brown paper bag
Tape or glue

You do: (See illustration.)
Cut off bottom of box.
Cut box in half lengthwise.

Child does: Covers outside of box half with brown paper.
Decorates with crayons, if desired.

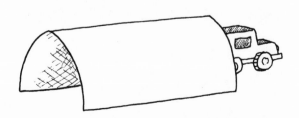

●■▲ MAILBOX

You need: Round oatmeal box with lid
Paper
Masking tape
Markers or crayons
Sharp knife
or optional flag: 1 two-pronged brass paper fastener
1 × 5 inch strip of cardboard

You do: (See illustration.)
Cut a 4–5-inch slot in the side of the box, for letters.

You and child do: Cover box with paper and secure seams and ends with masking tape. Cut through paper at slot.
Write child's name on sides of box.
Write "U.S. Mail" on the lid and tape lid to box at bottom only, so that lid opens and closes.
If desired, make mail flag using 1 × 5 inch strip of cardboard and a square of red paper. Use two-pronged fastener to tightly attach it to box.

▲　　　　**SPACE PACK**

You need:　Round oatmeal box with lid
　　　　　　Aluminum foil
　　　　　　Clear tape and masking tape
　　　　　　White paper
　　　　　　Scissors
　　　　　　Crayons or markers
　　　　　　Long sash, ribbon, or cloth belt (to go around child's
　　　　　　　chest)

You and　　(See illustration.)
child do:　Cover sides of box with aluminum foil and secure
　　　　　　with clear tape. Top and bottom of box can be
　　　　　　covered with foil or left plain.
　　　　　　Cut two slits in side of box and thread belt through.
　　　　　　Trim edges with masking tape. Decorate with paper
　　　　　　cutout buttons and instrument panels, labels (e.g.,
　　　　　　"Moon Mission" or "NASA").
　　　　　　Essential astronaut supplies can be stored and carried
　　　　　　inside box (flashlight, snack, etc.).

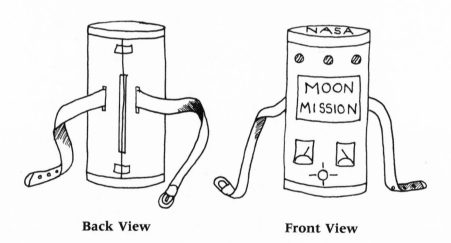

Back View　　　　　　**Front View**

▲ SPACESHIP

You need: Round oatmeal box (lid not needed)
Aluminum foil
Clear tape and masking tape
2 paper or Styrofoam plates
1 paper or Styrofoam cup
Scissors
Markers or crayons
Red or orange paper (optional)—crepe paper stream-
ers or long construction paper strips

You and   (See illustration.)
child do: Tape inverted cup to bottom of oatmeal box to form
nose cone.

Cover sides of box with aluminum foil, using extra
foil to cover base of nose cone. Tape in place, and
run a strip of masking tape around the foil on the
nose cone to give it a finished edge.

Cut centers out of two paper or Styrofoam plates,
large enough so that the remaining circles fit
around the oatmeal box at the base and about 2
inches higher. Tape in place with clear tape.

From the plate centers, cut four triangular fins about
5 inches long on the side to be taped to the
spaceship. Space evenly around the sides of the
ship and tape in place.

Optional—Long red or orange strips of paper may be
taped inside the hollow spaceship at the bottom, to
simulate flames.

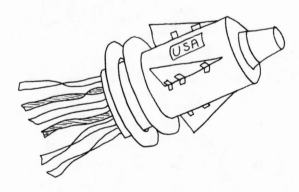

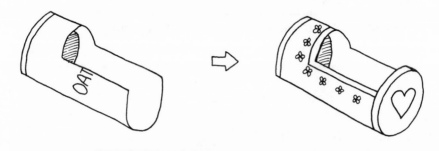

●■▲ STUFFED ANIMAL OR DOLL CRADLE/ TIME CAPSULE

You need: Round oatmeal box with lid
Paper (construction, white, or gift wrap)
Clear tape or masking tape
Heavy scissors or knife
Markers or crayons

You do: (See illustration.)
Remove lid and cut 7 inches into box, 6 inches across, and 7 inches back.

You and child do: Put lid back on cut end of box and tape securely with two layers of tape.
Cover outside of box with paper, trimming edges with clear or masking tape. It is not necessary to cover the box lid and bottom.

Child does: Decorates cradle with markers or crayons.
Inside of cradle can be padded with scrap fabric, a hand towel, or a homemade pillow.

Variation: If covered with aluminum foil and set on end, this cradle becomes a Time Capsule.

TIME CAPSULE

45

●■▲ DRUM

You need: Round oatmeal box (lid not needed)
Recycled gift wrapping paper or construction paper
Heavy scissors
Clear tape
Masking tape
Ribbon or string about 25 inches long

You do: (See illustration.)
Cut about 2½ inches off top of box, to make box
about 6½ inches high

You and
child do: Cover sides of box with wrapping paper. Secure with
clear tape and then reinforce and trim with strips
of masking tape around top and bottom edges and
in *X* pattern on sides.

Punch two holes near the bottom of the box and
thread ribbon through. Measure so that child can
hang drum from neck while marching, and tie.
(Knot will be invisible if tied inside box.)

Use spoons (or xylophone mallets) for drumsticks.

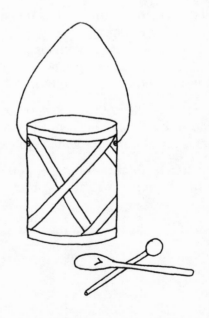

●THER BOX IDEAS

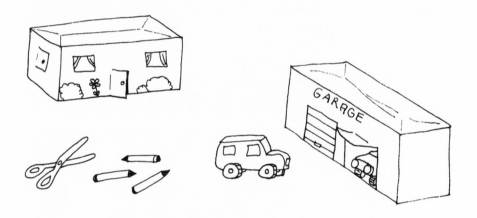

●■▲ BOX BUILDINGS

You need: Small-to-medium box (shoe box, tissue box, etc.)
Scissors
Paper (white or construction)
Tape or glue
Markers or crayons

You and
child do: Cover outside of box with paper. Bottom of box is
ceiling.
Cut out windows and doors. (Cut on three sides
only, so that they can open and close.)
Draw bricks, bushes, doorknobs, etc.
Child can draw on inside walls, glue on paper
furniture, put tiny toys inside, etc.

▲ DIORAMAS

These are especially nice when made using a theme such as a holiday, a special trip, or a recent book idea. See *Ideas* below.

You need: Small-to-medium box (A shoe box is a nice size.)
Scissors
Tape or glue
Crayons, markers
Construction paper
Extras: cotton balls, string, thread, aluminum foil, etc.
Clear plastic wrap (optional)

You and (See illustration.)
child do: Child decides on the theme of the diorama.
Set box on its side. Bottom of box will be the back of the diorama.
Using any or all of the materials mentioned, create a colorful background and floor for the diorama (i.e., cotton balls for snow, blue paper for ocean, black paper for night sky, etc.).
Add three-dimensional objects. Hang tiny birds, sun, airplanes, etc., from top of diorama, using thread. Glue other objects to floor or background.
Final touch (optional): Cover front of diorama with clear plastic wrap and secure with tape, to make a "window."

Ideas: Winter diorama: Cotton balls for snow, blue paper background with yellow paper sun and cotton clouds. Three cotton balls for snowman. Three-dimensional paper house.
Spring diorama: Light-blue paper sky, green paper for grass. Paper cutouts for flowers, sun. Cotton-ball clouds. Cotton-ball bunny with paper ears.
Ocean or Aquarium: Blue paper background. Hang paper fish, seaweed, seagulls, etc. Add real shells or rocks.
Desert: Tan paper floor, blue sky background. Paper cutouts of cactus plants, mesas, sun. Add real twigs. Play-dough lizards and snakes.

Mountains: Blue sky background with green or brown mountains. Paper birds hanging from ceiling. Paper trees. Add real twigs, grass, leaves.

City: Building cutouts with drawn windows. Paper traffic signs, billboards. Real toy cars or trucks.

Zoo: Animal cutouts with twigs for trees. Black paper bars for cages.

Halloween: Black paper background. Hang paper ghosts, witches, pumpkins, bats, full moon.

Christmas: Paper Santa, paper tree with ornaments, cotton snow, tiny paper gifts.

Chanukah: Paper menorah with paper candles of different colors. Aluminum foil for flames.

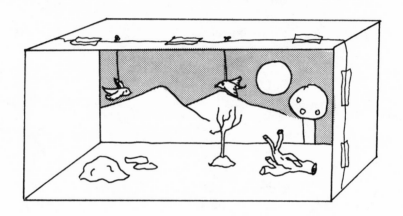

■▲ SHOE BOX COMPUTER AND DISK DRIVE

You need: Shoe box with lid
White paper
Black paper
White paper plates (2 or 3)
Black marker, crayon, or pencil
Scissors
Tape

You and (See illustration.)
child do: Cover box lid with white paper.

You or child write in keyboard symbols, circling each letter, number, arrow, etc., to represent *keys*. This can be accurate (copied from a typewriter or computer keyboard) or pretend (just the alphabet, for instance).

Cover the sides of the box with white or black paper.

Cut a 4-inch horizontal slit in one end of the box. This is the *disk drive*.

Make *disks* out of 3 × 3 inch squares cut from the center of paper plates (or other heavy-weight paper). Cut a hole in the center of each. Color them black on both sides. Use white paper to make disk envelopes. Store disks inside computer.

Draw wires on inside of box and lid.

Monitor can be separate pad of white paper.

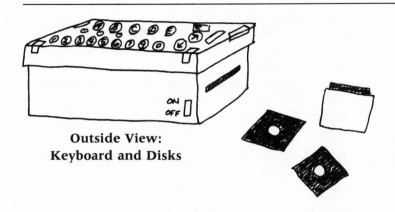

Outside View:
Keyboard and Disks

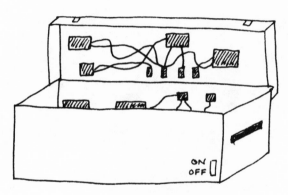

Inside View:
"Wiring"

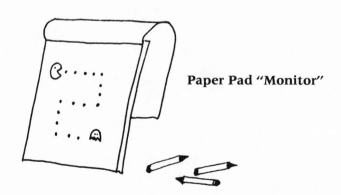

Paper Pad "Monitor"

●■ CAR/ROCKET SHIP/BOAT

You need: Box big enough for child (or stuffed animal) to sit in
Markers or crayons
Tape
Pot lid with center knob handle
Paper
Scissors

Child does: Decides whether vehicle is for him/her or a stuffed animal.
Decides what type of vehicle to make.
Designs and constructs vehicle with adult help when needed.

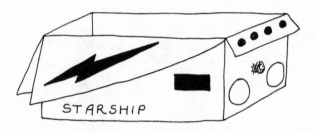

Outside View

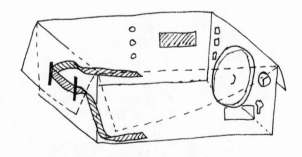

**Inside View of Steering Wheel
and Back View of Seat Belt**

You and	(See illustration.)
child do:	Steering wheel—Using scissors, punch a hole in driver's end of the box, just barely big enough for the pot lid knob to go through. Shove the knob through the box so that the lid is on the inside, as a turnable steering wheel.
	Using paper cutouts and crayons or markers, decorate vehicle with headlights, door handles, switches, instrument panel, etc.
	If desired, doors, windows, or spy holes may be cut in box. Box flaps can be cut to resemble rocket fins. Make a cardboard key to go in an ignition slot.
	Through two slits cut in the back of the box, a seat belt (long sash or old necktie) can be installed.

●■ TUNNELS

You need:	Large box or boxes Scissors or knife
You do:	Cut tunnel shapes large enough for child to crawl through in two or more sides of an inverted box.
Child does:	These tunnels are great for a game of Follow the Leader, an obstacle course, or pretend adventures. Two or more tunnels are the most fun. They can be spread out or taped together to make one long tunnel.

●■▲　PLAY HOUSE

You need:　Giant cardboard box (Find them at unfinished-furniture stores or appliance stores.)
Scissors or knife
Markers or crayons
Paper
Tape

You do:　As child directs you, cut a door, windows, peephole, etc. Child may want to draw windows on the box, and then you cut them out.

!　Do not allow child inside box while you are cutting windows!

Child does:　Designs and decorates house with paper curtains, pictures on the wall, Keep Out sign, Welcome mat, etc.
Sleeping bag or blanket on the floor and lots of stuffed animals are always welcome.

Variation:　If a giant box is unavailable, make, decorate, and furnish a cardboard box clubhouse for a favorite doll or stuffed animal.

PROJECTS
~ AND ~
# ACTIVITIES

■▲ RAINBOW CRAYONS

You need: Broken crayon pieces—all colors
              Muffin tin
              Aluminum foil

You do: Preheat oven to 300° F.
              Line each muffin cup with a separate piece of foil.

Child does: Takes all paper off crayons.
              Breaks crayons into 1-inch pieces (approximately).
              Puts crayon pieces into each foil-lined muffin cup.
                (Cups should be about half full of loosely piled
                crayons.)

You and   Put muffin tin in preheated oven and time for about
child do: 5–7 minutes. Watch *carefully,* since they melt
              quickly. Do not melt them completely—just
!   enough to blend them all together.
              Carefully remove from oven and allow to cool
              completely, in the muffin tin, without shaking the
              tin (about 30 minutes).

Child does: When completely cool, removes from tin and peels
              off foil. Crayons will be prettier on the foil side
              than on the top.

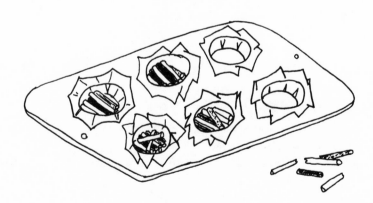

● ■ ▲   **PLAY DOUGH**
(This makes a wonderful, soft dough!)

You need: Medium-sized pot
Metal spoon for stirring
Wax paper
1 cup white flour
1 cup water
2 teaspoons cream of tartar
¼ cup salt
1 tablespoon vegetable oil
Food coloring (omit to make white dough)

You and child do: Put all ingredients in pot. Let child decide color of play dough.

! Cook over moderate heat, stirring constantly. Dough will eventually become harder to stir and will gather on spoon. At this point, dump the dough onto wax paper, allow to cool somewhat, and knead it until it is smooth (about 30 seconds).

Note: Store cooled play dough in a plastic bag. Requires no refrigeration.

■ ▲   **WAX PAPER AND CRAYON MELT**

You need: Crayons—all colors
Crayon or pencil sharpener
Wax paper
Newspaper
Iron
Scissors

You and child do: Put a sheet of wax paper on several thicknesses of newspaper.
Sprinkle shavings from crayon sharpener onto wax paper.
Top with another sheet of wax paper.

! Cover with another sheet of newspaper and iron with a warm iron until the crayon shavings melt.
Trim edges of wax paper with scissors, cutting to desired shape.
Tape on a sunny window.

58

●■▲ CON-TACT PAPER AND LEAVES

You need: Clear Con-Tact paper (self-adhesive paper, available in hardware and department stores)
Autumn leaves, ferns, flower petals, grass, etc.
Scissors

Child does: Collects leaves.
Arranges leaves on one sheet of Con-Tact paper (sticky side up).

You do: Cover leaves with second sheet of Con-Tact paper, smoothing out air bubbles.
Trim Con-Tact paper with scissors.

Child does: Hangs leaf project in a sunny window.

Indoor Variation: Instead of leaves, sprinkle tiny colored paper circles (from a paper punch), colored paper scraps, magazine pictures, glitter, etc., on the Con-Tact paper for a more opaque paper collage.

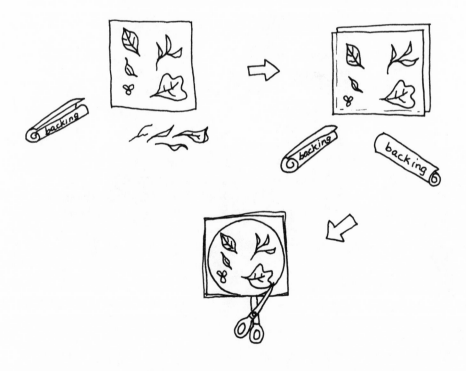

■▲   **COLLAGES**

You need: Background material—Can be almost anything: paper, Styrofoam meat trays, wood, cardboard box lids, shoe boxes, heavy tin foil, etc.

Collage materials—You can use dry foods such as beans, popped or unpopped popcorn, peas, macaroni elbows, shells, or wheels. Have your child collect things from around the house like Styrofoam packing pieces, cut-up drinking straws, colorful paper cups or plates cut into small pieces, bits of yarn or string, buttons, pictures from magazines or catalogs. Especially fancy items can be beads or "jewels" from broken yard-sale jewelry. For a Nature Collage, go outdoors and find twigs, leaves, tiny pebbles, acorn tops, seed pods, feathers, etc.

Glue—A small amount of glue poured on a square of aluminum foil or a paper plate and applied with a toothpick or Popsicle stick is less messy and less apt to flood than an overturned glue bottle.

Child does: Collects or prepares collage materials.
Glues materials to backing.

Ideas: Random gluing: Very young children will enjoy the simple pleasure of gluing objects to the backing.

Yarn outlines: An older child can make patterns or designs by gluing yarn or string to the backing to form shape outlines. The outlines can then be filled in with assorted collage materials.

Multi-media: Child can draw a simple picture on backing and then glue collage materials to drawing. (Real buttons on drawing of clothes; real feathers on drawing of bird; cotton snow falling on crayon winter scene.)

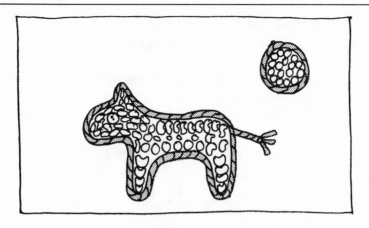

YARN OUTLINES

MULTI-MEDIA

■▲ PRINTING WITH PAINT

You need: Finger paint or poster paint
Paper
Printing objects (see *Ideas* below)
Paper towel

Note: Child should wear a smock or old shirt with the sleeves rolled up. The work surface should be protected against spills and overenthusiastic printing.
If child is in a highchair, tape the paper to the highchair tray so it doesn't move around during printing.

You do: Pour small amount of paint on a dish.
Make blotter out of paper towel folded into small square.
Tape down blank piece of paper, if desired.
Prepare potato printer, if necessary.

Child does: Collects objects to print with.
Dips printer object in paint, blots briefly, and prints!

Ideas: Potato prints: Cut potato in half and carve a shape or letter, or just gouge random holes in cut surface.
Block prints: Plastic or wooden blocks with alphabet or pictures.
Plastic (washable) toys, corks, pieces of sponge.
Elf feet (see illustration): Use the outside of your fist for the foot, and thumb and fingerprints for the "toes."
Thumbprint pictures (see illustration).
Paint with cotton swabs for a change of pace.

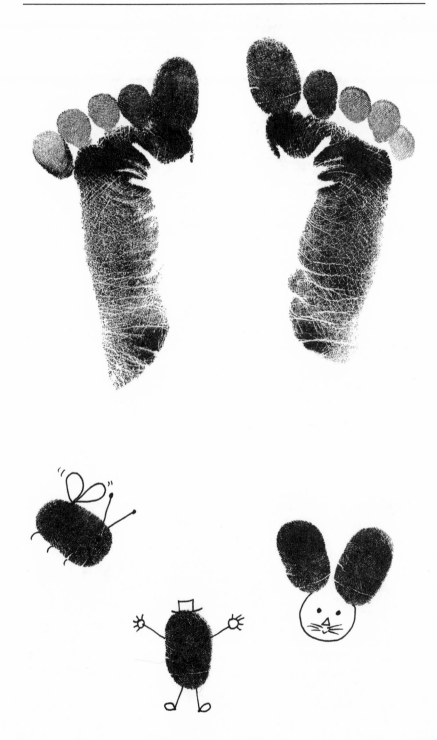

63

■▲ CRAYON/PAINT RESIST

You need: White paper
Crayons
Watercolor paints

Child does: Draws a crayon picture on the paper. The picture can be fancy or simple, or even scribbles. Just be sure child pushes *hard* with the crayon, so that the coloring is *heavy.*

Paint over the crayon drawing with watercolors. Try a blue wash for the sky and green for grass, or any colors at all. The crayon drawing will resist the paint and come through, bright and clear.

▲ *Idea:* Child can make a Mystery Message by writing a short message (or drawing a simple picture) on white paper using a white crayon. Be sure to press *hard* with the crayon.

Mystery Message is discovered only after painting paper with dark watercolor paint!

●■ SNOW ON A TRAY

This is a winter activity for indoors. It comes in handy on a snowy day when your child is too sick or too little or you are too busy to go out. It is great for a toddler in a highchair. Child can even wear jacket and mittens to add to the "outdoor experience."

You need: Cookie sheet, large baking dish, or large plastic box
Snow (soft is best)
Mittens
Miscellaneous toys (see *Ideas* below)

You do: Fill cookie sheet with large mound of snow.

Ideas: Small toy people can climb the mountain of snow or hide in carved-out snow caves.
Make a flag for the mountaintop, using a paper triangle taped to a toothpick or drinking straw.
Make a miniature snowman. (Use cut drinking straw pieces for arms, eyes, nose, buttons.)
Tiny toy boats can steer around icebergs.

■▲ CUP WALKIE-TALKIES

You need: 2 paper cups
Long string
Pencil

You do: (See illustration.)
Using pencil point, punch *small* hole in center of each cup bottom.
Thread string through and knot each end so string won't pull out.

You and child do: Walk apart until string is taut but not touching any corners or furniture.
Send and receive messages: Child puts cup over ear as you speak or whisper into your cup. Then you listen as child speaks into cup. (You might mention that "the sound waves travel along the tight string.")

▲ SUPER BUBBLES
(This is an outdoor activity.)

You need: Quart container
½ cup liquid dish detergent (Joy works best)
Liquid glycerine (optional—available at drug stores)
Drinking straws (2 for each person)
String (about 30 inches per person)
Flat-bottomed basin

You and
child do:
Pour ½ cup detergent into quart container.

Add enough water to fill container.

Add 1–3 teaspoons of liquid glycerine (optional).

Pour mixture into basin so that it is about ½ inch deep.

Thread string through two drinking straws and tie ends together (see illustration).

Holding one straw in each hand, with straws together, dunk the straws and string into the bubble liquid. Gently lift the straws and string out of the liquid and pull the straws apart. There should be a big rectangular bubble formed by the straws and string. Now, walk backward (or pull your arms back) so that the bubble catches some wind and bulges out. At this point, bring the straws together again to close the bubble.

After some practice, the giant bubbles should float free.

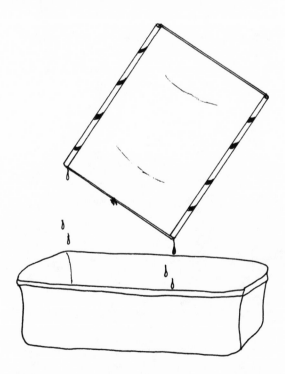

▲ EGGLOO VILLAGE

You need: White eggshell halves that are fairly intact (no big cracks)

Shoe-box lid or other piece of cardboard to use as base

Cotton balls

Glue

Pencil

Aluminum foil

Play dough (optional)

You do: Wash eggshells and let dry.

You and child do: (See illustration.)

Glue foil over one area of base, for ice and water. (Or water can be blue paper.)

Glue pulled-apart cotton balls to base for snow, leaving water and ice uncovered.

With pencil, draw bricks on eggshell halves. Big chips can be eggloo door. If shell breaks, smaller domes can be storage eggloos or doghouses. Position eggloos on snow.

Make play-dough figures to populate village (e.g., people, dogs, sled, canoe or kayak, fish, etc.).

CARDBOARD TUBE CRAFTS

●■▲ BINOCULARS

You need: 2 cardboard tubes from toilet-paper rolls
Aluminum foil
Masking tape
String or ribbon (about 2 feet long)

You and child do: (See illustration.)
Cover tubes with foil.
Secure and trim ends with masking tape.
Tape tubes together at ends.
Punch two holes at one end of binoculars and tie on
string or ribbon to hang from child's neck.

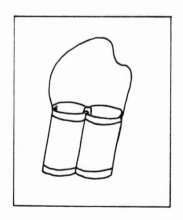

● ■ ▲ **TELESCOPE**

You need: Cardboard tube from paper-towel roll
Aluminum foil
Masking tape

You and Cover tube with foil.
child do: Secure and trim ends with tape.

● ■ **LONG STRAIGHT PIPES/LONG CROOKED PIPES**

You need: Lots of cardboard tubes (Long gift-wrap tubes are
best; also use paper-towel and toilet-paper tubes.)
Masking tape
Scissors
Small ball or marble

You and (See illustration.)
child do: For long straight pipe, use masking tape to connect
tubes.
For crooked pipes, cut tubes or tube ends at an angle
and tape together with masking tape.
For either type of tube, the *longer* the better.

Ideas: Send a small ball or marble through tube, back and
forth.

● ■ Use tube as a Whisper Tube for secret messages.
Child listens at one end of tube as you whisper a
message. Then child whispers message as you
listen.

■ ▲ Also try **Kazoo,** page 99.

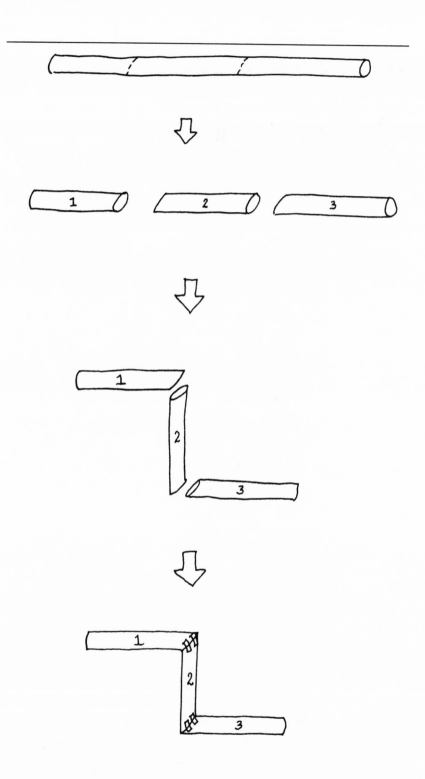

EGG-CARTON CRAFTS

The egg-carton crafts described below all require roughly the same supplies. These are:

> Cardboard egg carton
> Scissors
> Crayon or markers
> Clear tape
> Clothespin for Clothespin Doll Skirt
> 2 pipe cleaners or toothpicks for Caterpillar

●■▲ INSTANT TEA SET

You do: (See illustration.)
Cut out the individual egg "cups" from the bottom of the carton. Trim and bend the edges of each cup to form handles for cups, or a spout for a pitcher.
You can also cut out small spoons from egg-carton scraps, if desired.

Child does: Decorates each item with crayons or markers. Sets table for tea party.

Note: If Styrofoam egg carton is used, this tea set can serve real "tea"!

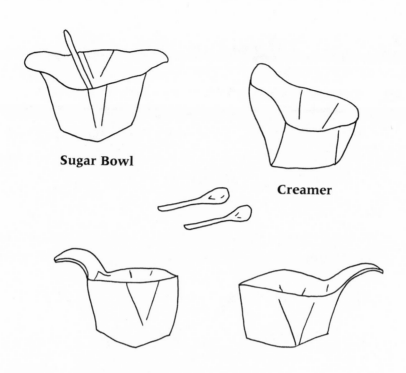

Sugar Bowl

Creamer

● ■ ▲   **DOLL HATS**

You do: (See illustration.)
             Cut individual cups from bottom of egg carton.

Child does: Decorates cup (hat) with crayons, markers, ribbon,
             colored paper, etc.
             Yarn can be attached to tie under doll's chin.

■▲ CLOTHESPIN DOLL SKIRT

You do: (See illustration.)
Cut cup from bottom of egg carton.
Cut clothespin-size hole in cup bottom (skirt top).

Child does: Decorates cup (skirt) with crayons, markers, etc.
Draws face and hair on clothespin.

■▲ CATERPILLAR

You do: (See illustration.)
Cut at least four (or more) connecting cups from carton bottom.

Child does: Draws face on one end of caterpillar.
Decorates the rest of caterpillar body with crayons or markers. Each section of body can be a different color.
Pushes two pipe cleaners or toothpicks into head, for antennae. (These can be colored with marker, if desired.)

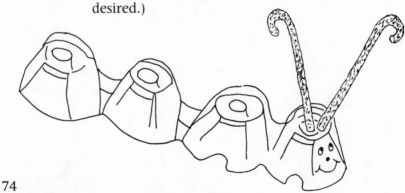

SCIENCE ~~~ PROJECTS ~~~

●■ SPOON REFLECTIONS

(A 10-second science discovery)

You need: A shiny metal spoon

You and   Have child look at his/her reflection in the bowl
child do: (concave side) of the spoon. The reflection will be
upside down.

When child looks at his/her reflection in the back of
the spoon (convex side), the reflection is right side
up.

Note: (See illustration.) The images are right side up or
upside down depending on the direction in which
the curved surfaces reflect light.

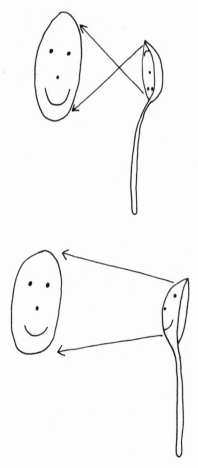

●■▲ MAGIC BALLOON

You need: Balloon
Small-mouthed bottle (small juice or soda bottle)
Baking soda
Vinegar
Funnel

You and child do: Using the funnel, have your child dump about 1 heaping tablespoon of baking soda into the balloon. (Use less if balloon is small.)

Using the funnel again, help your child pour about 1–2 inches of vinegar into the bottle.

Being careful not to dump any baking soda into the bottle, stretch the balloon over the top of the bottle. While you hold the balloon *tightly* to the top of the bottle, have your child straighten the balloon, letting the baking soda fall into the vinegar.

Note: The gas formed by mixing vinegar and baking soda will inflate the balloon!

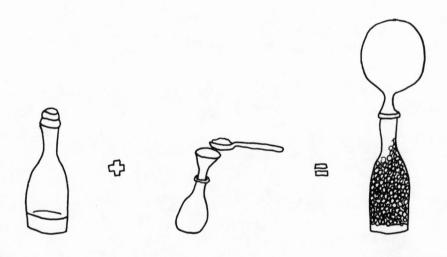

●■▲ BALLOON ROCKET ON A STRING

You need: Balloon (The bigger the balloon, the longer the flight.)

Long, thin, smooth string (Kite string works well.)

1 drinking straw

Tape

You and child do: (See illustration.)

Secure one end of string at far end of room.

Standing at other end of room, thread loose end of string through straw.

Blow up balloon and pinch it closed, so air doesn't escape.

Tape inflated balloon to straw.

Hold string taut and let go of balloon.

Balloon will shoot across the room on the string.

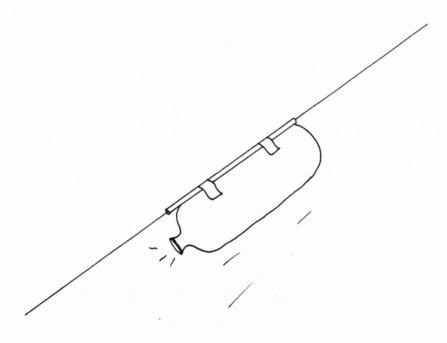

▲ CORNSTARCH AND WATER

You need: ¼ cup cornstarch
Water—2 tablespoons plus a few extra drops
Bowl
Spoon

You and child do: Pour ¼ cup cornstarch into the bowl. Add 2 table-spoons of water and stir till blended. As you blend, the mixture will get "strange." It will flow like a liquid, but will also break or crumble like a solid. (You may have to add a few more drops of water for the mixture to flow.)

Scoop some up in your hands. You have the right consistency if the mixture is liquid when cupped in your hand, but is solid when you play with it and squeeze it.

■▲ WATER AND OIL

You need: Clear glass jar with cover
Cooking oil
Water
Food coloring (optional)

You and child do: Pour about ½ inch of oil into jar. Add 2 inches of water. Show child how the oil floats on top of the water.

Cover jar and let child shake mixture up. Watch how oil and water separate.

Add a few drops of food coloring (not yellow). Shake again and watch the results.

●■▲ SWIRLING COLORS/MIXING COLORS

You need: Clear glass jars or drinking glasses
Water
Food coloring

You and
child do:
Fill a glass with water.

As child watches through the side of the glass, add 2–3 drops of food coloring to water, one drop at a time. If water gets too colored, start again with fresh water, slowly adding different colored drops.

Rinse glass and refill with water. Have your child count the drops as you slowly add about 5 drops of blue food coloring. Stir. Now add 5 drops of yellow food coloring, stir, and ask your child to tell you what's happening to the water.

Start again with fresh water and this time use 5 drops of red food coloring, stir, and add 5 drops of yellow. Let your child choose the colors to mix, and try to predict what colors he/she will get.

Then, try mixing colors a slightly different way. Put ½ cup of water and 5 drops of blue food coloring in one glass. Add ½ cup of water and 5 drops of red food coloring to another glass. Add 1 cup of water and 10 drops of yellow food coloring to a third glass.

Ask your child what will happen when you pour half the yellow water into the red water. What will happen when you pour the rest of the yellow water into the blue water?

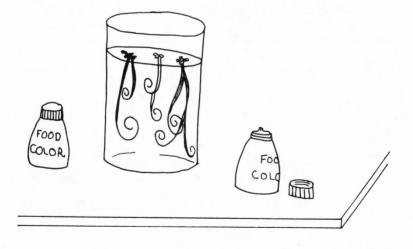

■ ▲　WATER MUSIC

You need:　4–6 tall drinking glasses, preferably the same size and shape

A metal teaspoon

You and child do:　(See illustration.)

Pour about 1 inch of water into the first glass.

Pour 2 inches of water into the second glass.

Pour 3 inches of water into the third glass, and so on.

When all glasses are ready, line them up, as shown, and tap each, gently, with the spoon. Adjust the tone of your water xylophone by removing or adding water.

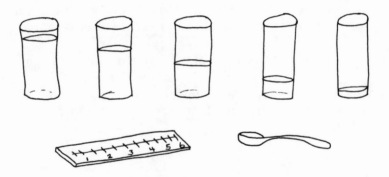

■▲ BALLOON MAGNET—STATIC ELECTRICITY

You need: Small- to medium-sized inflated balloon (Long, hot dog–shaped balloons work best.)
Coarse pepper sprinkled on a plate
A dry day

You and child do: Rub balloon in hair for about 15 seconds.
Place balloon on wall. Balloon should stick to wall because of static electricity.
Rub balloon in hair and then lift slowly from head. Static electricity from balloon will make short hair stand on end.
Rub balloon again, and hold about 1–2 inches over plate of pepper. Pepper will dance around and jump up to adhere to balloon.
To clean balloon, wash with water.

▲   **JUMPING FLAME**

You need: Candle in a holder
                Matches

You do: Remind child to be careful of the candle and the
                flames.

!   Light candle and let it burn for about 2 minutes.
                Light a match.
                Ask child to blow out candle
                Immediately hold the lit match *in the trail of candle
                smoke,* about 1–2 inches from the wick. The flame
                will jump to the wick and relight the candle.

Note: The more smoke, the better this trick works. (The lit
                match ignites the vapors rising from the smoking
                candle wick.) The candle can be magically relit
                again and again and again . . .

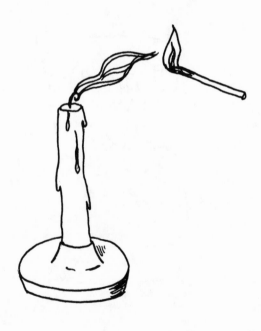

●■▲　CANDY SPARKS

You need:　Wint-O-Green Lifesavers candy
Pliers
Clear plastic bag
A totally dark closet

You do:　Hold one Lifesavers candy with the pliers.
Put the plastic bag around the pliers and candy, so that the "exploding" candy won't fly all over the closet.

You and　Get comfortable in a dark closet.
child do:　Squeeze the candy with the pliers, hard enough to break it. As the candy breaks, you will see a flash of light.

Note:　This demonstrates a strange phenomenon called *triboluminescence*, which is light produced when certain crystals are crushed.

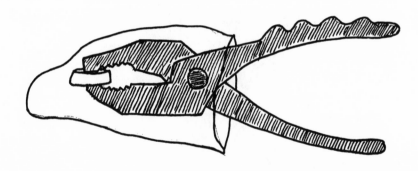

●■▲ RAINBOW CELERY—A BEDTIME ACTIVITY

You need: 1 leafy stalk of celery
2 glasses or glass jars
Sharp knife
Water
Food coloring

You and child do: Using knife, cut ½ inch off bottom of stalk to expose new edge.

Starting 2 inches below the leaves, split the celery stalk down the middle.

Fill each glass with water and add a different food color to each until colors are *very* bright. (Red and blue are good.)

Put one half celery stalk in each glass. Go to bed.

In the morning: The separate colors will have climbed up the celery stalk and colored the leaves. This shows how plants drink water through their stems.

●■ FIRST WORDS SCRAPBOOK

You need: Colorful magazine pictures
Either "magnetic" photo album *or* heavy paper bound into a book with yarn or string.

You do: Fill book with magazine pictures of:
- people—man, woman, girl, boy, baby, etc.
- objects—car, shoes, tree, flower, pot, apple, etc.
- animals—dog, cat, fish, squirrel, bug, etc.
- actions—run, kiss, hug, bathe, jump, sleep, etc.
- familiar faces—snapshots of Mom, Dad, sister, brother, relatives, friends.

With masking tape and permanent marker, label each picture (or whichever pictures you choose) with a one- or two-word description (e.g., "girl," "run," "big bear").

You and child do: This book can be a lasting favorite for your child. The very young child will enjoy looking at the pictures with you and identifying the objects, people, actions, and ideas. Later, the child will be able to point to the label and read the word appropriate to the picture.

●■ CUTOUTS TO CATEGORIZE

You need: Lots of magazine pictures of individual people or things (You can store them in a big envelope.)

You and child do: Have child categorize pictures in different ways:
- Put all the pictures of people together.
- Put all the pictures of food together.
- Put all the pictures of animals together.
- Put all the pictures of toys together.

●■ **WHAT'S MISSING?**

You need: Paper
Crayon, marker, or pencil

You do: Draw a simple picture with something missing:
- A house with no door.
- A face with no nose.
- A glove with only three fingers.
- A car with no tires.

You and child do: Ask the child to identify what's missing, and then to finish the picture.

●■ BEGINNER MIND PUZZLES

You need: Paper
Crayon, marker, or pencil

Ask child to:
- Draw a triangle.
- Draw a square.
- Draw a circle.
- Draw a circle inside a square.
- Draw a triangle with a circle around it.
- Draw a square with three little circles inside it.

Make up more puzzles of your own.

▲ TRICKY PUZZLES
(for the older child)

Ask child to: • Draw five squares using only six lines.

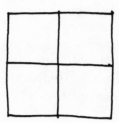

• Draw two squares using only six lines.

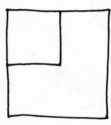 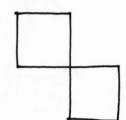

• Draw one square and two triangles, using only five lines.

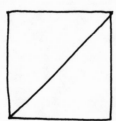

- Draw this house figure without lifting your pencil from the paper!

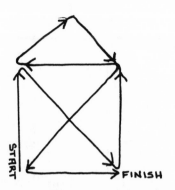

Ideas: Make up your own puzzles *or* have your child make up some to try on *you.*

Child can memorize a puzzle and test adults.

▲ **SIMPLE CROSSWORD PUZZLE**

You need: Paper and pencil

You do: Construct a very simple crossword puzzle, using short words and familiar clues.

Tips: (See examples on following pages.)

Make a grid pattern (6 × 8 spaces is a good size). Fill in the words first. Start with a couple of long words and build from them. It helps to start in the middle of the grid and work outwards.

Finally, make the child's copy (empty grid with numbered squares). Black out the unused spaces. List the clues.

You and child do: Child uses the clues to solve the puzzle. Either you or your child can fill in the answers.

CROSSWORD PUZZLE EXAMPLE #1

		¹T	O	²Y	S
³B	A	A		E	
		B		S	
⁴B	A	L	L		⁵C
E		E			O
A			⁶B	I	B
R			O		
⁷S	C	H	O	O	L

ACROSS

1. You like to play with ____.
3. What does a lamb say?
4. What do basketball, baseball, football and tennis all use?
6. If you spill your soup, you should wear a ____.
7. You learn a lot when you go to ____.

DOWN

1. Before we eat, we have to set the ____.
2. The opposite of *NO* is ____.
4. Teddy ____are cute.
5. Do you like to eat corn-on-the- ____?
6. When you want to surprise someone, you yell, ____!

94

CROSSWORD PUZZLE EXAMPLE #2

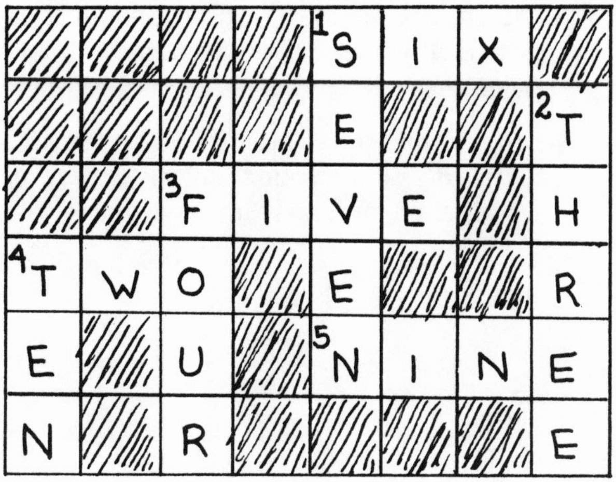

				¹S	I	X	
				E			²T
		³F	I	V	E		H
⁴T	W	O		E			R
E		U		⁵N	I	N	E
N		R					E

ACROSS

1. 4 + 2 = _____
3. 5 + _____ = 10
4. 8 − 6 = _____
5. 7 + 2 = _____

DOWN

1. 6 + 1 = _____
2. 5 − 2 = _____
3. 3 + 1 = _____
4. 6 + 4 = _____

▲ EARLY READING BOOK

You need: Small spiral notebook (a used one with only a few pages left is ideal), or a homemade book of blank pages.

You do: Write a simple story (one or two sentences per page) using *only* words your child can *already* read. If this is only three or four words, use one word per page.

Child does: Illustrates each page appropriately.
Reads the book with *no help!*

Joe ran fast.

He saw a big dog! "Hi, dog!" said Joe.

Other **Writing and Thinking** ideas are found in the **Quiet Games** section, page 139. Try **Free Association, Opposites,** or **Guessing Games.** Also, try **Cooperative Picture,** page 16.

INSTANT MUSICAL INSTRUMENTS

■▲ KAZOO

You need: Cardboard tube from toilet-paper or paper-towel roll
5 × 5 inch square of wax paper
Rubber band
Sharp pencil
Crayons or markers

You and child do: (See illustration.)
Cover one end of cardboard tube with wax paper and secure with rubber band. Wax paper should be *tight* across end of tube.
Using pencil point, poke a *small* hole in the center of the wax paper.
Using pencil, poke a ¼-inch hole midway on the cardboard tube.

Child does: Decorates cardboard tube with crayon or marker.
Hums into open end of tube.
Uses fingers to cover and uncover large hole in tube, while humming, to change the sound.

●■▲ SHAKER

You need: Nonbreakable closed container—film cannister, empty plastic medicine bottles with child-proof caps, small yogurt containers (heavy-weight plastic kind), small cardboard boxes
Dry beans, rice, macaroni, pebbles, buttons, etc.
Heavy tape
Colored paper and crayons (optional)

You and child do: Put a small amount of dry beans (or whatever) into container.
Cover container and tape closed.
Decorate shaker with colored paper and designs.

●■▲ DRUMS

You and   Make Oatmeal Box Drum (see page 46).
child do: *Or*

Thread a ribbon or string through the hole in a
muffin tin, cookie sheet, or cooling rack, and child
can march while drumming.

Or

For a sit-down performance, use an assortment of
pots and lids, metal bowls, an inverted muffin tin,
and a wire cooling rack for different sounds.

Note: Use real drumsticks or try spoons (wooden ones are
quieter than metal) or xylophone mallets.

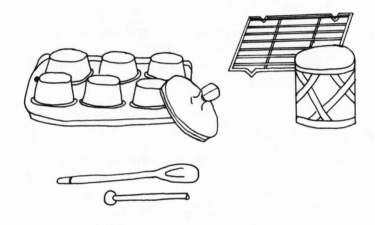

●■▲ HARP

You need: Styrofoam (or cardboard) meat or vegetable tray; or shoe-box lid

4–8 rubber bands (Different sizes and widths are best.)

Child does: (See illustration.)

Decorates inside of tray with crayon.

Stretches rubber bands around tray, spacing them about 1 inch apart. If desired, arrange rubber bands in order of tone.

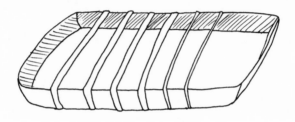

■▲   Also try **Water Music,** page 82.

COOKING

QUICK AND EASY

▲ **PEEL A CARROT**

You need: Long carrot
Vegetable peeler

You do: Remind child to scrape carrot *away* from himself or
!   herself to avoid getting cut.

Child does: Peels carrot with or without adult supervision. This
can often take quite a while. . . .

Ideas: Eat carrot like a bunny.
Make carrot sticks and dip. (Easy dips are peanut
butter, cottage cheese, cream cheese.)
Make a salad plate (carrots, celery, green pepper,
olives, etc.).
Make hors d'oeuvres. Slice carrot into circles and top
each circle with a small slice of cheese, or a dab of
peanut butter topped with a raisin, etc.

■▲ COLORED EGGS

You need: Hard-boiled eggs (room temperature)
Crayons or markers

Child does: Decorates eggs with designs, faces, scribbles, flowers.

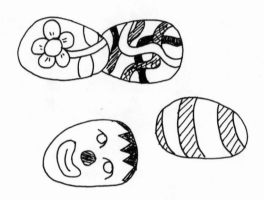

■▲ CELERY STUFFERS

You need: Celery sticks, washed and dried
Any or all of the following: peanut butter, cream cheese, cottage cheese, raisins, nuts, sunflower seeds
Butter knife

Child does: Spreads the desired filling on celery. Tops with raisins, nuts, or seeds.

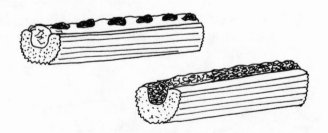

● ■ ▲ **LUNCH DESIGNS**

You need: Lunch fixings for your child

You do: (See illustration.)
Create a scene or design using your child's lunch.

Ideas: Cut sandwich into house shape. Use a carrot circle and thin carrot sticks for sun, and cheese pieces for doors and windows.

Cut sandwich into robot shapes. Use raisins for eyes and buttons.

Cut sandwich into sailboat shape. Use pretzel sticks for mast, fish-shaped crackers for fish, cottage cheese for clouds.

Plate is face with round crackers topped with peanut butter and raisins for eyes, cheese for nose, carrot stick for mouth, apple slices for ears.

FACE

SAILBOAT

HOUSE

ROBOT

▲ **APPLE VOLCANOES**

You need: Apple
Peanut butter
Raisins
Knife
Teaspoon

You do: Cut off top of apple.
Using spoon, scoop out core of apple.

You and
child do: Fill apple with peanut butter and top with raisins.

Note: If this is to be eaten later, brush apple edges with lemon juice to prevent browning and wrap in foil.

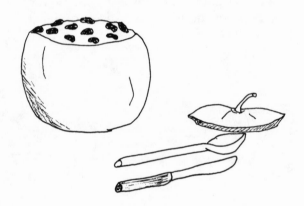

●■▲ BANANA POPS

You need: Banana
Popsicle stick
Honey
Wheat germ, in a shallow dish
Teaspoon

You and child do: (See illustration.)
Cut banana in half.
Push Popsicle stick into cut end of one banana half, about 1½ inches deep.
Peel banana half.
Drip a *little* honey on banana and gently spread over banana surface with back of spoon.
Roll honey-coated banana in wheat germ until banana is covered.

●■▲ PEANUT BUTTER CANDY

You need: 1 cup smooth, unsweetened peanut butter
1 cup powdered milk
½ cup honey
1 teaspoon vanilla
½ cup shredded coconut (optional)
½ cup raisins
About 50 chocolate chips, M & M's, or raisins

You and child do: Mix all ingredients together in a large bowl.

You do: Roll mixture into balls about 1 inch in diameter. Flatten each ball slightly and put on wax paper on a plate.

Child does: Puts chocolate chip, raisin, or M & M in center of each ball.

Note: Chill. Store, covered, in refrigerator. Makes about 50 candies.

■▲ **FRUIT KABOBS**

You need: Any favorite fruits, fresh or canned: strawberries, banana chunks, grapes, bite-sized chunks of cantaloupe or watermelon, apple slices (brush with lemon juice to prevent browning), canned pineapple chunks, canned peach slices, etc.
Wooden skewers (available in supermarkets)

You and child do: Thread colorful and tasty assortment of favorite fruits on skewers.
Eat right away, or cover with plastic wrap and refrigerate for later.

Note: Be sure to snap off sharp skewer points after making
!   kabobs.

■▲ SALAMI AND CREAM CHEESE HORS D'OEUVRES

You need: 4 salami or bologna slices (3 inches across or bigger)
Cream cheese (Cheese at room temperature spreads more easily, but this is not essential.)
Butter knife
Sharp knife
Toothpicks (optional)

Child does: (See illustration.)
Spreads cream cheese on three slices of salami.
Stacks spread slices of salami on top of one another.
Tops stack with last slice of salami.
Presses gently with hand, to slightly compress salami-and-cheese stack.

You do: Using sharp knife, slice stack into eight wedges, as shown.

Child does: Inserts toothpick in each wedge.

Note: These are a tasty and fun snack for a party or any time. Chill in refrigerator if not eaten right away.

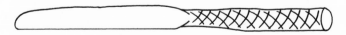

FROZEN TREATS

●■▲ **FROZEN BANANA SLICES**

You need: A banana
Butter knife
Paper plate

Child does: Peels banana.

!   Cuts banana into slices, each about ¼ inch thick (assist with cutting if necessary), and puts slices on plate.

You and Freeze.
child do: Eat like candy!

●■▲ FROZEN GRAPES

You need: Seedless grapes

Child does: Picks grapes off bunch and puts on dish.

You and child do: Freeze.
Eat frozen grapes like candy!

■▲ FROZEN BANANA FLUFF

You need: About ⅓ pound tofu
1 banana, cut up
½ cup smooth, unsweetened peanut butter
1 heaping tablespoon of honey
Food processor or blender

You and child do: Put all ingredients in food processor or blender. Process until mixture is smooth.
Cover cookie sheet with wax paper or aluminum foil. Drop mixture by spoonfuls (globs) onto cookie sheet. *Or* spoon all mixture into clean heavy-weight plastic bag. Snip off one corner and squeeze mixture onto cookie sheet forming sticks, circles, or letters.
Freeze.
When Banana Fluff is frozen, wrap each stick in foil and store in freezer for quick, yummy, and nutritious frozen snacks!

■▲ YOGURT AND FRUIT POPSICLES
(A nice change from plain juice Popsicles!)

You need: Plain yogurt
Fruit (bananas, strawberries, blueberries)
Honey
Popsicle molds (or small paper cups) and Popsicle sticks
Blender or food processor

You and child do: For every measuring cup of yogurt, add ¼–½ cup fruit, and honey to taste.
Blend until smooth.
Pour into Popsicle molds or paper cups.
Insert Popsicle sticks.
Freeze.

■N THE OVEN

▲ PUMPKIN SEEDS

You need: Pumpkin or squash seeds

You and child do: Wash and remove pulp from pumpkin or squash seeds.
Soak seeds for a few hours (or overnight) in salty water (optional).
Drain and spread seeds on cookie sheet.

! Bake in preheated 325° F oven for about 20 minutes until golden brown. Store in airtight container.

●■▲ NACHOS

You need: Tortilla chips, pita bread triangles, or bread triangles
Cheese
Toppings, if desired: sliced olives, sour cream, etc.

You do: Preheat oven to 350° F.
Slice cheese into thin pieces that will fit on tortilla chips.

Child does: Spreads tortilla chips on cookie sheet.
Puts cheese slices on each chip.

! *You do:* Bake 5 minutes, or until cheese is melted.

Child does: Adds toppings.

115

●■▲ TINY PIZZAS

You need: English muffin, split
Spaghetti or tomato sauce
Mozzarella cheese (or any favorite cheese), shredded
Toppings: sliced or chopped veggies (green pepper, onion, mushrooms); sliced ripe olives; sliced hot dogs; tiny salami wedges; pepperoni; etc.

You and child do: Preheat oven to 350° F.
Put opened English muffin on shallow baking tray.
Spread about 1 tablespoon of sauce on each muffin half. (Omit sauce if child doesn't like it.)
Sprinkle with 1–2 tablespoons of shredded cheese.
Child can add favorite toppings.
Bake at 350° F for 10 minutes, until cheese melts.

!

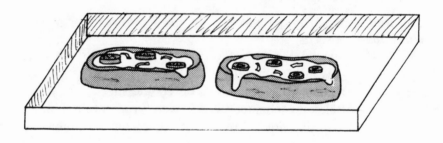

●■▲   GRANOLA

Your child can do most of the measuring, adding, and mixing of ingredients.

You and   Preheat oven to 250° F.
child do: Mix the following ingredients in a large pot:

> 3 cups rolled oats
> ¾ cup raw sunflower seeds
> ¼ cup raw wheat germ
> ¼ cup raw sesame seeds
> 1 cup shredded coconut
> 1 cup walnuts, almonds, or cashews, broken up

Add:

> ½ cup vegetable oil
> ½ cup honey
> ¼ cup hot water

Stir until ingredients are moistened.

! Spread mixture on cookie sheets and roast in 250° F oven for about 1 hour, stirring occasionally, until golden brown. When cool, add 1 cup raisins (or other dried fruit).

■▲ CORNBREAD

Your child can do most of the measuring, adding, and mixing of ingredients. This is a good group recipe, since everyone can have a chance to add an ingredient to the bowl.

You and
child do:

Preheat oven to 425° F.

Mix in a large bowl:

1¼ cup cornmeal
½ cup white flour
¼ cup whole wheat flour
¼ cup brown sugar
2½ teaspoons baking powder
½ teaspoon salt

Add:

1 egg
1 cup milk
3 tablespoons vegetable oil

Beat until smooth.

Bake in greased 9-inch square pan in 425° F oven for 20–25 minutes. *Or* make muffins and bake for about 15 minutes.

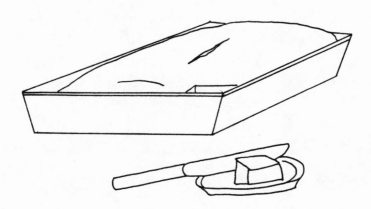

■▲ PUMPKIN MUFFINS

This is another good group recipe. Each child gets to add an ingredient or two to the mixing bowl, and baking time is short. These muffins are moist and tasty. You might try them as an alternative to cupcakes at a party.

You and   Preheat oven to 350° F.
child do: Mix in a large bowl:

> 2 cups white flour
> 1 cup whole wheat flour
> 2 cups sugar
> 4 eggs
> 1 cup vegetable oil
> ½ teaspoon cinnamon
> 2 teaspoons baking powder
> 2 teaspoons baking soda

Add and beat in:

> 2 cups (one 15-ounce can) pumpkin

Fold in:

> 1 cup chopped walnuts
> 1 cup chocolate chips (or you can add raisins instead)

Grease muffin tins or line with paper baking cups. Bake at 350° F for 20–25 minutes.
Makes 34–36 muffins.

119

～～PRETEND～～

PUPPETS

●■ PEANUT-SHELL FINGER PUPPETS

You need: Peanut shells that fit on your finger
Fine-tipped markers

You and child do: Draw faces and hair on shells and have a puppet show. (Don't forget to eat the peanuts!)

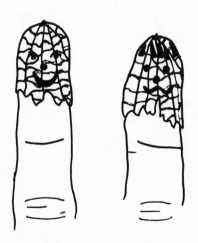

▲ STICK PUPPETS

You need: Pictures of people (Snapshots of the family are especially fun, but you can also use drawings on stiff paper or magazine pictures.)

Pictures or drawings of animals, the sun, a cloud, etc., depending on the puppet show theme.

Scissors

Drinking straws

Clear tape

You and child do: Cut out the pictures in the shapshots, drawings, or magazines (full figures or heads only).

Tape each cutout to the top of a drinking straw to make a stick puppet.

■▲ SOCK PUPPETS

You need: An old sock
Fabric scraps (Felt is best.)
2 buttons
Needle and thread (or glue)
Yarn scraps
Marker or pencil
Paper-towel roll (optional)

You and (See illustration.)
child do: Have child put sock on hand (thumb in heel of sock
for lower jaw) and mark position of eyes, nose,
tongue, hair, etc., with marker.
Put paper-towel roll inside sock, to prevent sewing
the two sides together.
Sew (or glue) buttons for eyes, yarn for hair, fabric
scraps for tongue and ears. Draw nostrils and
eyebrows with marker. Puppets can be people,
animals, monsters, etc.

■▲ PUPPET SHOWS

Stages

Supersimple stages are made from furniture. Turn a coffee table on its side. *Or* drape a cloth over a table or a chair and hold puppets up from behind.

Ideas: Nursery rhymes: For example, "Hickory Dickory Dock" with a mouse puppet and a drawing of a tall clock; "Jack and Jill" with two puppets, a hill made from a blanket thrown over a chair, and a tiny bucket cut from an egg carton.

Stories: Might be from favorite books, TV, or made up.

Family rituals or special events: For instance, bedtime, meals, going to school, visits from relatives, or a birthday.

Songs: Old favorites like "Mary Had a Little Lamb," "Old MacDonald," or "Itsy, Bitsy Spider."

Jokes: For instance, two puppets telling "knock-knock" jokes or riddles.

COSTUMES

■▲ FIREFIGHTER

Ideas:
Newspaper Hat (see page 3) worn with pointed end back. Tape aluminum foil to front of hat and tape a black paper "#1" onto the foil.

Child wears raincoat and boots.

Make an aluminum foil badge and tape to raincoat.

Hose made of cardboard gift-wrap tube or paper-towel tubes taped together.

■▲ PRINCESS/PRINCE

Ideas: Paper crown: Decorate with colored jewels.

Royal necklace/medallion: Thin cardboard or foil circle, decorated with colored-in paper jewels. Punch hole and thread with ribbon.

Royal belt: Waist-length aluminum foil, folded until it's about 1½ inches wide. Decorate with taped-on paper jewels. Put on child and tape closed in back.

Royal cape: Tie or pin a towel.

Princesses might like some royal lipstick and blush.

■▲ SUPERHERO

Ideas: Belt: Waist-length aluminum foil, folded to 1½-inch width and held on with tape.

Emblem: Aluminum foil or paper emblem taped to child's shirt. (A paper plate is a good thickness for an emblem.)

Wrist cuffs: Aluminum foil, old sock tops, or paper cups with the bottoms cut out.

Cape: Tie or pin a towel.

Child can wear tights with contrasting color knee socks over them.

▲ ASTRONAUT

Ideas: Belt: Waist-length aluminum foil, folded to 1½-inch width and held on with tape.

Wrist cuffs: Aluminum foil, old sock tops, or paper cups with the bottoms cut out.

Paper-bag helmet, decorated with dials.

Oatmeal Box Space Pack (see page 43).

If desired, Robot-type paper-bag costume (see page 132).

Big, heavy gloves.

●■ PAPER BAG TURTLE

You need: Brown paper grocery bag
Scissors
Black marker or crayon

You and   (See diagram.)
child do: Cut off side of bag that has writing on it.
In bottom of bag, cut U-shaped hole for child's neck.
In each side of bag, just around the corner from the bag bottom, cut U-shaped holes for the child's shoulders.
Draw a turtle-shell pattern on the blank and uncut side of the bag.
Child wears costume while on hands and knees, crawling slowly! Tape sides to child's shirt to secure if necessary.

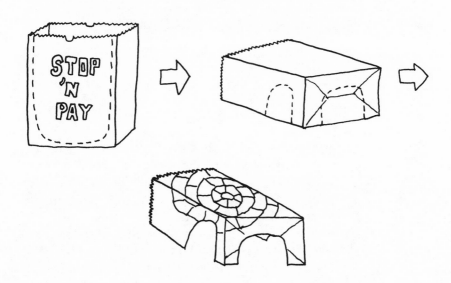

●■ ANIMALS

Ideas: Tail: Cut open a brown grocery bag so that it is a large rectangle. Roll up the long way (crumpling as you roll is okay), making a roll about 36 inches long. Tape around roll in several places. At one end, cut a 6-inch fringe through all thicknesses (cut a few at a time). Flatten and soften roll and cut it if it's too long for child. Tape or safety pin unfringed end to child's pants.

Fur: Inside-out sweatshirt and sweatpants.

Paws: Dark socks on hands and feet.

Eyebrow pencil whiskers and black nose.

Cardboard "bone."

Folded blanket on the floor for a bed.

Teach "animal" tricks—sit, roll over, jump, etc. Then put on a show.

▲ INDIAN VEST AND HEADBAND

You need: Brown paper grocery bag
Colored paper
Scissors
Crayons or markers
Tape

You and child do: Headband: Cut 2-inch strip from top of bag for headband. Measure and cut to fit child's head. Decorate with Indian symbols (see below). Cut feathers from colored paper and tape on headband where desired. Tape to fit child's head.

Vest: (See diagram.) Cut up the middle of the printed side of the bag. Cut off bottom of bag, so you now have a long rectangle. Trim so that rectangle is about 34 × 15 inches (to fit child better). Fold ends in so that they meet in the middle. (Have writing *inside* vest.) Cut armholes along each fold, about 2 inches from top of bag. Cut V-shape in front of vest. Cut fringe on bottom of vest, all around.

Decorate with Indian symbols.

130

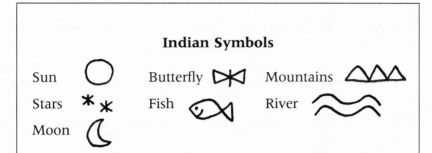

Indian Symbols

Sun ⬭   Butterfly ▷◁   Mountains △△△

Stars ✳ ✳   Fish 🐟   River 〜〜

Moon ☾

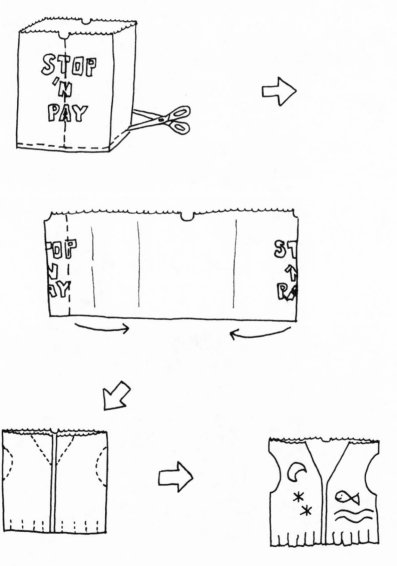

■▲ ROBOT

You need: Brown paper grocery bag
Aluminum foil
Colored paper
Scissors
Tape
2 paper-towel or toilet-paper rolls (optional)

You and   Slit grocery bag up middle of blank large side. Cut
child do: neck hole in bottom of bag. Cut armholes in sides.
Cover front of bag (with writing on it) with aluminum foil. Secure with tape.
Decorate with colored-paper buttons, switches, and
dials.
Make aluminum foil headband and decorate with
paper dials.
For stiff robot arms, slit two paper-towel rolls lengthwise. Decorate with crayon, marker, or paper and
put over child's arms.

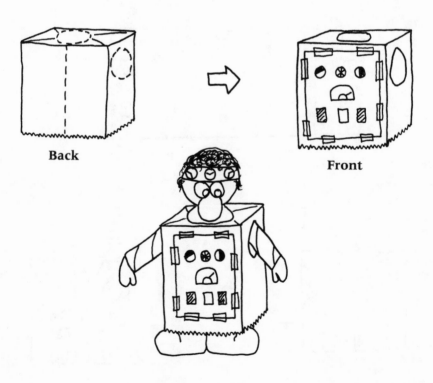

Back

Front

132

PRETEND PLACES AND ACTIVITIES

●■▲ INDOOR CLUBHOUSE, TENT, OR FORT

Super Simple

Throw a couple of old sheets or blankets over a table or chairs to make soft walls and a ceiling.

Rearranged Furniture

Line up chairs to make a wall. Set sofa cushions on their sides on the floor to form other walls. Cover with a blanket.

Hang a Tent

(See illustration on following page.) String a long piece of cord from one end of a room to the other, about 3–4 feet off the floor. Hang an old sheet or blanket across the cord and pin each end to the cord with safety pins. Then, using more pins, cord, and secure "anchors" in the room (doorknobs, hooks, tops of heavy furniture), erect a tent.

Child does: Fills with books, pillows, stuffed animals, and a sleeping bag for pretend camping, a snack, or a nap.

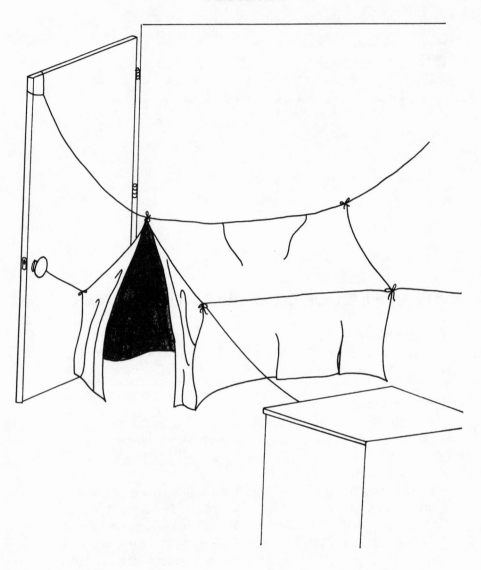

■▲   BEAUTY PARLOR/BARBER SHOP

This is a good time for a shampoo, haircut or trim, manicure/pedicure, or new hairstyle. Call the child "Sir" or "Madam," be very cordial, and carry on a lively conversation, inquiring about the child's family, job, politics, etc.

■▲   RESTAURANT

This is especially nice at lunch time. Either you or your child (or both of you) make a menu with reasonable choices of food and drink. Child can be waiter/waitress, cook, and customer, or just customer. If child is waiter/waitress, don't forget to leave a tip!

●■▲ AEROBICS CLASS/WORKOUT GYM

Good exercise for both you and your child. Child can wear T-shirt and shorts, tights and leotard, or sweats. A headband of some sort and sneakers complete the outfit. Put on some lively music and take turns leading the exercises.

■ FISHING

Make a fishing pole using about 2–3 feet of string tied to the end of a chopstick, dowel, or cardboard gift-wrap tube. Make a hook using a pipe cleaner, a bent paper clip, or cardboard cut into a hook shape. Make "rainbow trout" out of paper—fish shapes colored with rainbows! Punch a small hole in each fish and scatter them on the floor. Child goes fishing and collects them on the hook.

GAMES

QUIET GAMES

■▲ First to Smile

Participants sit across from each other and stare at each other silently. The first person to smile loses the game.

●■▲ First to Laugh

Same as First to Smile, except that first person to *laugh* loses the game. No talking or tickling is allowed, but you can make lots of silly faces at your opponent.

●■▲ First to Look Away

Players sit across from each other and stare into each other's eyes. First person to look away loses the game.

■▲ Free Association

You say a word and child responds with the first word that comes to mind.

Examples: boy—girl
snow—cold

■▲ Opposites

You say a word and child responds with the opposite. Or you *act out* a word and child acts out the opposite.

Examples: sleep—awake
stand—lie down
cry—laugh

●■▲ Guessing Games

Decide on a category before the game starts (e.g., animals, objects, people, places). You think of a word in the category and give clues, one at a time, while child tries to guess the word. Then switch around and have child think of a word and give you clues.

Example: Category is Animals. Child tries to guess after each clue is given.

Clue #1: "I'm thinking of an animal that lives in the forest."
Clue #2: "This animal has a long, bushy tail."
Clue #3: "This animal's fur is reddish orange."
Clue #4: "This animal can be very sneaky or sly."
The answer is "a fox."

●■▲ "I See Something Red"

From where you are sitting, spot an object of a particular color and announce, "I see something (color)." The child guesses objects of that color until he/she guesses the correct one. Then the child chooses an object of a certain color and you have to guess.

●■▲ Tabletop Hide-and-Seek

This is best done on a somewhat crowded table. Choose a small object (a small piece of paper, a marble, a button, a paper clip, etc.) and show it to your child. While child's eyes are closed, hide the object on a cluttered table. Be sure to hide it in such a way so that things don't have to be lifted or moved around (to avoid spills). Ask your child/children to find the hidden object, without touching anything on the table.

This miniature game of hide-and-seek works well in a doll house too!

■▲ Tong Transfer (Quiet Version)

Using kitchen tongs (two-handed technique for little hands), transfer small toys or kitchen items from one bowl to another.

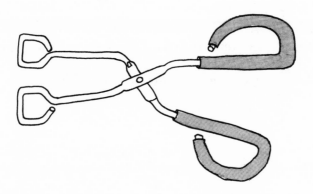

■▲ Spaghetti Threader Game

(See illustration.) Stand a strand of uncooked spaghetti in a small lump of play dough. Have child thread Cheerios, one by one, onto the spaghetti without breaking the strand. (You can break the strand in half to make the job quicker.)

This can also be a group contest or game. Children can count the Cheerios on their spaghetti strands after a timed period of threading.

■▲ Tabletop Memory Game

Spread a selection of five to ten small objects on the table. (These can be anything. If you're at a restaurant or in a waiting room, use items from your handbag, pockets, etc.)

Have your child study the objects. Then clear them away or cover them up. Ask your child to list as many objects as he/she can remember, as you write them down (or produce the item).

■▲ Also try **Cooperative Picture,** page 16.

GAMES FOR TIME IN THE CAR

●■▲ Color Hunt

Choose a color and watch out the window for objects of that particular color. Whenever the child sees one, he/she says, "I see an orange (object)!" Try to list ten objects before choosing a new color.

If two or more kids are in the car, they can compete to see who gets ten objects first, *or* they can cooperate to get ten objects together, with an adult keeping score.

●■▲ Yellow Car/Red Car

Choose a color and watch for a car of that color. Whoever spots the car first calls out, "(Color) Car!" and then gets to choose a different color for the next car.

■▲ Alphabet Hunt
Watch out the window for road signs, billboards, store signs, etc. Children call out the letters of the alphabet, in order starting with *A*. (Young children will need help with this.)

■▲ Number Hunt
Watch out the window for numbers from 1 to 9, in order.

●■▲ Scavenger Hunt
This is a good game for long drives. Give child/children lists of things to watch for during the drive. Children can cooperate or compete to see who can find all the items on the lists.

The lists can be made up ahead of time or during the drive, and adjusted for the type of scenery and the age of the children.

Scavenger Hunt Examples:

CITY LIST
Flashing red light
Bus
Sign in a foreign language
Dog
Grocery store
Railroad tracks
Playground
Billboard with child on it
Billboard with cat on it
Police officer

RURAL LIST
Silo
Railroad tracks
Post office or school
Cows
Dirt road
Pond or lake
Tractor
A fence
Gas station
Horses

SUBURBS LIST
School
Flashing traffic light
Grocery store
Person on a bicycle
Statue
Church
Playground
Flower garden/snowman
Children
Pickup truck

● TODDLER LIST
Tall building
Lake or pond
Person on a bicycle
Bridge
Red car
Animal
Truck
Stop sign
Store
Person wearing a hat

●■▲ Also try **Guessing Games,** page 140.

144

WHILE YOU WAIT

Supersimple and instant ideas for restaurants and waiting rooms.
You can carry paper and pencils (or pens) with you, use the backs
of paper placemats, paper napkins, or (in an office) ask a
receptionist for supplies.

ACTIVITIES

These require paper and pencil and are described elsewhere in
this book. Paper placemats are a convenient paper source!

- ●■▲ *Snappy Puppet Mouths* (See page 4.)
- ●■▲ *Small-Scale Tracing* (See page 14.)
- ●■▲ *Small Object Rubbings* (See page 13.)

■▲ *Cooperative Picture* (See page 16.)
■▲ *Beginner Mind Puzzles* (See page 91.)
▲ *Tricky Puzzles* (See page 92.)

WAITING GAMES

■▲ Letter Search

Using a paper placemat with advertising (or whatever) on it, pick a letter and have the child/children search for the letter and circle it as many times as it appears.

▲ Word Search

Using a paper placemat with advertising (or whatever) on it, pick a common word and have the child/children search for the word and circle it as many times as it appears.

●■▲ "Guess What I'm Drawing"

Using the blank side of a paper placemat (or your own paper), slowly draw a familiar person, object, or shape. Child/children guess as you draw, trying to guess the outcome of the picture before you are finished. Then, reverse roles and have a child draw the picture.

●■▲ Color Hunt

Pick a color and ask child/children to search the room for objects of that particular color.

●■▲ Shape Hunt

Pick a simple shape (square, circle, triangle) and ask child/children to search the room for objects of that shape.

● Tabletop Change-Around

Good game for very young children at a restaurant, before the food arrives.

Arrange four spoons in a row in the center of the table. Have the child study them for a minute and then close his/her eyes. Change the position of one of the spoons (e.g., turn it over, take it away). Ask the child what changed on the table. Repeat with any other objects on the table, making more subtle changes for older children.

●■▲ Hide the Penny

This game uses two or three of those little plastic cream containers that restaurants serve with your coffee.

Empty the containers, remove the foil covers, and dry with a napkin. Hide a penny under one container and invert the other two containers on the table. Move the containers around and then ask the child to point to the one that has the penny under it.

Note: Play this game at home using two or three identical paper cups.

ACTIVE GAMES AND PARTY GAMES

These are active games that can be played indoors. Many of these games are good for groups of children or for parties.

●■ Be an Animal
Children act out animal movements. Each child can have a turn choosing an animal that everyone should be.

▲ Charades
On slips of paper, write or draw simple ideas for children to act out, keeping within one category. Children take turns acting out an idea, while the other children guess what it is.

Examples: Animal charades: dog, cat, snake, monkey, elephant, bunny, snail, mosquito

Sports charades: basketball, tennis, baseball, swimming, skiing, gymnastics, hockey

Story charades: Goldilocks, Sleeping Beauty, Pinnochio, Little Red Riding Hood

Activity charades: fishing, cooking, sleeping, reading a book, getting dressed, patting a dog

●■ Do What I Say/Do What I Do
Either an adult or a child is leader and leads group through a series of body movements. This can be done silently through actions only, or with verbal cues.

Examples: Lie down on your back.

Raise one leg up and down.

Raise one arm up and down.

Stand up and clap your hands two times.

Jump up and down three times.

Try to touch your toes.

Touch your head, shoulders, knees, and toes.

▲ Simon Says

More advanced version of Do What I Say. Children do only the action that "Simon says" to do.

■▲ Make a Letter

Children lie on the floor and form letters of the alphabet with their bodies. This can be done in a group, as you call out the letter, or each child can make a letter while the others guess what it is.

●■▲ Follow the Leader

Make an obstacle course with cardboard-box tunnels (see page 53), sofa cushions, and rearranged furniture for line of children to walk, crawl, and scramble through.

■▲ Treasure Hunt

With children in another room, hide a large number of small objects (candies, peanuts, pennies, buttons) all over a room. Children come in together and hunt for objects, collecting them in bags.

■▲ Tong Transfer (Active Version)

Using kitchen tongs to pick up and carry small objects, children take turns carrying items from station to station. A large group can be split into two teams to race against each other. (This requires two pairs of kitchen tongs.)

■▲ Indoor Bowling

A collection of toilet-paper rolls set on end serve as pins. The bowling ball is tennis ball size or smaller.

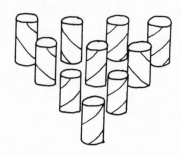

▲ Scoop Catch

Make scoops: (See illustration). Cut the bottom 2 inches off a plastic one-gallon milk jug. Wash it out and dry it. Held upside down, this makes a great scoop for games of catch.

The "ball" can be any soft, safe object: foam ball, bean bag, small stuffed animal, pair of rolled-up socks.

Throw the ball to the child, who must catch it in his/her scoop. The child can also try to throw it back to you using only the scoop.

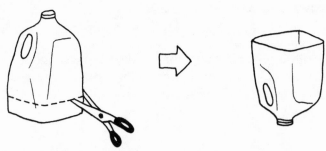

▲ Scoop "Hot Potato"

This is a party game in which each child has his/her own scoop. The children sit in a circle and pass a foam ball, bean bag, or tiny stuffed animal from one scoop to the next while music plays. When the music stops, whoever has the ball in his or her scoop sits in the middle of the circle (or gets to help operate the music).

●■▲ Balloon Basketball (Active or Quiet)

This game is harder than it sounds. Have children line up behind a piece of masking tape on the floor and take turns tossing a balloon into a laundry basket or hamper. A big balloon is especially fun because it floats and bounces more. For young children, an adult can be stationed near basket to "rebound" missed shots and help them into the basket. Don't forget to cheer!

Balloon basketball can also be played by a child confined to bed. The child uses a small balloon, aims for an empty wastebasket or basin positioned at the foot of his/her bed, and has an adult handy for rebounding.

●■▲ Also try **Bean Bag Games,** page 34. (Bean bags are nice party favors!)

WORK

It's a good feeling to know you're needed and that your help is worthwhile. Here is a list of simple chores that will enable young children to help out at home, be with you, and feel proud.

●■▲ Kids do windows!
Use *water* in a spray bottle and *one* paper towel or rag.

■▲ Empty wastebaskets

●■▲ Laundry
Child can help sort dirty clothes (dark from light) or clean clothes (e.g., "Find all the socks and match them up," or "Find all of your clothes and put them in a pile.")

●■▲ Category pickup
A more interesting way to clean up the house or playroom: "Pick up all the red things." "Pick up all the square things." "Pick up all the things made of wood." "Pick up all the books."

■▲ Dust the furniture

▲ Sweep the floor
Child can use a broom or a whisk broom.

■▲ Set the table
Napkins, utensils, and nonbreakable dishes only!

▲ Unload the dishwasher or dish drainer
Utensils and nonbreakable dishes.

■▲ Rake leaves/Shovel snow
Child-size rakes and shovels are nice, but not essential. This job usually turns into play as soon as there's a pile of leaves or snow to jump in.

●■▲ Help in the garden
Planting flowers or vegetables is fun and exciting, and child can take (limited) responsibility for the plants throughout the season by weeding and watering.

FREE
~~~ TRIPS ~~~

When all else fails, getting out of the house often does wonders for everybody's mood. But it's easy to fall into the habit of ending up at the shopping mall, wandering aimlessly through stores, buying toys and snacks for nagging children. Try to make trips a special experience by visiting new places, meeting new people, and doing new things.

Here are some trips you might try with your children. They are simple, free, and refreshing.

●■▲ Library

Your local library probably has a schedule of events including story hours, movies, and craft days for children. Larger libraries lend records as well as books. Spend an hour browsing, reading the magazines and books, and then take some home.

●■▲ Local Farm/Pet Store

Local farms are often happy to have visitors. You can tour the horse and cow barns, see the sheep, and admire the pigs!

Pet stores are like miniature zoos with lots of dogs, kittens, rabbits, hamsters, guinea pigs, birds, fish, and snakes. Visit the store and then draw pictures of favorite animals.

●■▲ Greenhouse/Florist with Greenhouse

Touring a greenhouse in winter is nicest of all, enjoying the warm and humid air, the green leaves, and the colorful flowers. You might want to buy seeds or a tiny plant to transplant at home.

●■▲ Museum

Large museums are often expensive, but smaller, local museums are either free or inexpensive. They're also uncrowded, easier to get to, and easier to get *through*.

■▲ Elementary School

With permission from the school secretary, you and your child can take a walk through your child's future school, admiring the art work on the walls or the exhibits in the display cases.

■▲ University Offices

If you live near a university, try visiting the Fine Arts Department for exhibits of paintings, sculpture, weaving, etc. Or try the

Entomology Department for cases of insect collections. The Geology Department might have exhibits of rocks, crystals, and geodes. Call ahead and ask.

You might even take a picnic if the campus has a good spot.

■▲ Restaurant, Factory, or Dairy Tour

Call ahead and find out if nearby restaurants, factories, or dairies in your area give tours for small groups of children. Fast-food restaurants are often happy to do this, and sometimes end the tour with a complimentary meal!

●■▲ Collector's Trip

Go for a walk around the block or up and down your street. Take a bag with you and collect any small, interesting treasures your child might find. Bring home seed pods, acorns, pretty leaves, flower petals, bottle caps, tiny pebbles, and "mystery objects" for a collage or treasure box.

●■▲ Rotten-Weather Walk

When the weather is so awful that only crazy people would go outside, dress for the weather and go outside! (Being out in a downpour is a change of pace, and the rain sounds great on a raincoat hood or umbrella.) You don't have to go very far for a "weather experience," and a cold drink to cool off or a hot drink to warm up will be a nice activity to go home to.

■▲ Puddle Jumping

After a good rainstorm, dress your child in a raincoat, *old* pants, and boots and go searching for puddles to jump in. If you do this in town, people may look at you strangely, but your child will have a ball. Then go home and change his/her clothes.

●■▲ Window-Shopping

If you live in a city or town, go on an outdoor window-shopping trip. (Let your child know ahead of time that you're not planning to buy anything.) Just about any store will have things in its windows that can spark a conversation between your child and you, and the walk in the fresh air is good exercise.

■▲ Art Gallery/Poster Store

Even an art gallery can be a good destination if you ask questions about the art that your child can relate to.

Examples: "Which picture is your favorite? Why?"

"Is that picture happy or sad?"

"Does that picture make you feel warm or cold?"

"Can you find the picture with the white house (puppy, red flower, etc.) in it?"

●■▲ Playground/Park

Of course, the playground or park is a wonderful destination for you and your child. To keep it from getting repetitious or dull, take different activities to do once you get there.

Examples: Take a picnic lunch or snack.

Take a kite.

Take paper and crayons to make leaf rubbings.

Take paper and crayons to draw what you see.

Take paper and crayons to draw a simple map of the area.

Take a book or game to read or play at the park.

Take a wet paper towel in a plastic bag, so your dandelions won't wilt before you get home.

Take bubbles and Super Bubbles (see page 66).

Take a bag to collect things for a Con-Tact Paper and Leaves collage (see page 59) or a Nature Collage (see page 60).

PARTY TIME AND PLAY GROUP ∿TIME∿

Many activities and crafts in this book are fun and easy for groups as well as for one or two children. Listed below are some ideas for party fun, or for a short, structured activity during a preschooler's play group.

Some of the games, crafts, and recipes that follow result in a take-home product for each child in the group. You and your child can make party favors ahead of time, or a craft can be a party activity producing a take-home treat.

DECORATIONS

■▲ **Party Decorations,** page 22
▲ **Japanese Lanterns,** page 24

MAKE-AHEAD PARTY FAVORS

■▲ **Sewing Cards,** page 30
Use 6 × 6-inch squares of white poster board. Draw a simple picture on each, using colorful markers. Write each child's name on his/her card. Cover with clear Con-Tact paper. Punch holes. Attach yarn.

●■▲ **Bean Bags,** page 34
Write each child's name on a bean bag with marker. Use for Bean Bag Games.

■▲ **Rainbow Crayons,** page 57

●■▲ **Play Dough,** page 58
Make three different colors. Give each child three golf ball–sized lumps of play dough in a small plastic bag.

PARTY FOODS TO MAKE AHEAD OF TIME

■▲ **Celery Stuffers,** page 106
●■▲ **Banana Pops,** page 109
■▲ **Fruit Kabobs,** page 110
■▲ **Salami and Cream Cheese Hors d'Oeuvres,** page 111
●■▲ **Yogurt and Fruit Popsicles,** page 114

● ■ ▲ **Frozen Banana Fluff,** page 113
● ■ ▲ **Pumpkin Muffins,** page 119

FOODS TO MAKE WITH A GROUP

● ■ ▲ **Banana Pops,** page 109
  ■ ▲ **Fruit Kabobs,** page 110
● ■ ▲ **Tiny Pizzas,** page 116
  ■ ▲ **Cornbread,** page 118
  ■ ▲ **Pumpkin Muffins,** page 119

PARTY CRAFTS TO TAKE HOME
(*Be sure to write each child's name on his or her crafts.*)

● ■ ▲ **Paper Fan,** page 12

  ■ ▲ **Paper Collage,** page 21
Have glue sticks and items to glue ready beforehand.

  ■ ▲ **Weaving Paper Placemats,** page 22
Cut slits in paper and have paper strips ready.

  ▲ **Berry Box Weaving,** page 38
Grocer can give you a stack of plastic berry boxes. Ribbon scraps are especially pretty for weaving.

● ■ ▲ **Con-Tact Paper and Leaves,** page 59 (See illustration.)
  Cut clear Con-Tact paper into 6 × 12 inch rectangles. Children collect leaves, flower petals, etc., in small bags. Peel the backing from *half* the Con-Tact paper rectangle and let children arrange leaves on the sticky surface. Peel off the rest of the backing and fold the Con-Tact paper over to seal in the leaves.

  ■ ▲ **Crayon/Paint Resist,** page 64

  ■ ▲ **Caterpillar,** page 74
Cut out strips of four egg-carton cups ahead of time.

Con-Tact paper with backing

12"

6"

David

backing

PARTY (OR PLAY GROUP) GAMES AND ACTIVITIES

●■▲ **Tracing Your Child,** page 16
Trace each child on a big piece of paper. Children color in their own faces and clothes, or draw amazing costumes.

■▲ **Cooperative Picture,** page 16
Tape a large piece of paper to a door, washable wall, or floor. (A 4-foot piece of freezer paper will do.) Children line up and take turns drawing a person, a scene, or whatever, making it as silly as they want to.

●■▲ **Bean Bag Games,** page 34
Children take bean bags home as party favors.

■▲ **Treasure Hunt,** page 149
Kids take home what they find (peanuts, M & M's, etc.)

■▲ **Spaghetti Threader Game,** page 141
●■ **Be an Animal,** page 148
▲ **Charades,** page 148
●■ **Do What I Say/Do What I Do,** page 148
▲ **Simon Says,** page 149
■▲ **Make a Letter,** page 149
●■▲ **Follow the Leader,** page 149
■▲ **Tong Transfer (Active Version),** page 150
■▲ **Indoor Bowling,** page 150
▲ **Scoop Catch,** page 150
▲ **Scoop "Hot Potato,"** page 151
●■▲ **Balloon Basketball,** page 151

PLAY GROUP TRIPS
(*Call ahead for permission, if necessary.*)

●■▲ **Local Farm Tour,** page 159
●■▲ **Greenhouse Tour,** page 159
●■▲ **Museum,** page 159
■▲ **Restaurant, Factory, or Dairy Tour,** page 160

INDEX

172